Professional Ethics

Combined text

AAT Diploma Pathway Unit 32

Jo Osborne

Roger Petheram

**osborne
BOOKS**

Published by Osborne Books Limited
Unit 1B Everoak Estate
Bromyard Road
Worcester WR2 5HP
Tel 01905 748071
Email books@osbornebooks.co.uk
Website www.osbornebooks.co.uk

Design by Richard Holt
Cover image from Getty Images

Printed by the Bath Press, Bath

British Library Cataloguing in Publication Data
A catalogue record for this book is available from the British Library

ISBN 1 905777 04 3

Contents

Acknowledgements

The authors wish to thank the following for their help with the production of the book: Sarah Fardon, Mike Gilbert, Jon Moore and Jenny Clarke. Thanks must also go to Trish Sayer of McKnights of Worcester for advising on current accounting practice and for providing standard letters used in the accounting process.

Lastly, the publisher is indebted to the Association of Accounting Technicians for permission for the reproduction of extracts from the Specifications for the Diploma Pathway, the Guidelines on Professional Ethics and the sample simulation which forms the basis of the second practice simulation in this book.

Authors

Jo Osborne is a Chartered Accountant who trained with Ernst & Young in their London office. She then moved to Cable & Wireless where she spent two years in their internal audit department before moving into an investment appraisal role. Jo has taught AAT at Hillingdon College and more recently at Worcester College of Technology where she teaches on all levels of the AAT qualification.

Roger Petheram has lectured at Worcester College of Technology on a wide range of accounting, business and management courses for a number of years. He previously worked as a senior accountant for the Health Service. He is currently senior editor for accounting texts at Osborne Books, with particular responsibility for the AAT Series.

Introduction

Professional Ethics has been written to cover the requirements of AAT Diploma Pathway Unit 32 of the same name.

Professional Ethics is a very practical book designed for use by students who need a guide to the subject which covers both theory and practice.

Professional Ethics has been written to expand on and explain the *AAT Guidelines on Professional Ethics*. This document is reproduced, by kind permission of AAT, in Appendix 1 of this book.

Professional Ethics is a 'combined text' which contains two main sections:

- A **tutorial section** containing seven chapters covering the Unit 32 performance criteria and 'knowledge and understanding' requirements. The chapters contain:
  - a clear text with many practical 'examples' which illustrate theoretical points
  - a chapter summary and key terms to help with revision
  - student activities – the answers to a selection of which are to be found at the back of this book
- A **practice simulation** section containing two full length simulations, the second of of which is based on the the AAT guidance simulation.

A note to tutors – Tutor Packs

The answers to the two simulations and selected student activities are available in a separate paper-based *Tutor Pack*. This data – together with the answers to the remaining student activities – is also available electronically on a CD. Please contact the Osborne Books Customer Services on 01905 748071 for details of how to obtain this tutor support material.

Osborne website

The Osborne Books website has proved popular for its free downloads and multiple choice quizzes. Log onto www.osbornebooks.co.uk and try us.

AAT website

Support material for Unit 32 for tutors and students is available on www.aat.org.uk, including the *Guidelines on Professional Ethics,* guidance on course delivery and interesting material on 'whistleblowing'.

this chapter covers . . .

The aim of this chapter is to introduce you to the principles of professional ethics. We will look at what 'professional ethics' means and describe the fundamental ethical principles that members of the AAT should follow. These principles are followed in 'Guidelines on Professional Ethics' published by the AAT.

Specific areas covered include:

■ *the fundamental principles of professional ethics*

■ *the people to whom these ethics apply*

■ *the reasons why professional ethics are necessary*

■ *the objectives of the accounting profession*

PERFORMANCE CRITERIA COVERED

unit 32: PROFESSIONAL ETHICS

This chapter introduces the main principles of professional ethics which are common to all three of the elements of Unit 32, and form part of the underpinning knowledge and understanding of the Unit.

Element 32.1:

apply general principles and procedures for ethical compliance expected within the accounting sector

A   *Identify and apply fundamental principles of honesty and integrity.*

B   *Highlight situations within professional work that require objectivity and fairness, and where judgements and actions could compromise personal or organisational integrity and reputation.*

C   *Recognise the principles of effective Continuing Professional Development (CPD) to maintain professional and technical competence (to include sources of advice and information outside formal learning).*

D   *Recognise and explain why certain types of information should be regarded as confidential.*

E   *Identify circumstances when it would be appropriate to disclose confidential information.*

F   *Identify the key issues which ensure professional services are performed within the scope of professional ethics guidance.*

G   *Make critical decisions to identify appropriate ethical behaviour when interacting with others in a variety of circumstances.*

H   *Refer and seek advice from relevant sources for issues beyond own <u>professional</u> competence.*

I   *Describe the types of contractual obligations you would have in providing service to clients to include due care and carrying out assignments within a reasonable timescale.*

J   *Discuss, agree and resolve any ethical conflict.*

AN INTRODUCTION TO PROFESSIONAL ETHICS

what are ethics?

Firstly, a definition:

The professional ethics of an organisation are the moral principles or standards that govern the conduct of the members of that organisation.

You may have heard people refer to the fact that a person or an organisation has done something that is 'unethical', or that they themselves wouldn't do something because it was unethical. For example, you would consider it unethical for a doctor to give information to a newspaper about the treatment given to a celebrity patient without the patient's consent.

So why do we feel that this is unethical on the part of the doctor? In this case the doctor would have broken patient confidentiality – ie released information that is 'secret' and 'private' to that patient – and the doctor's actions would be considered unethical because of this.

Members of professional bodies are expected to maintain the standards of their organisation. As part of this they are expected to behave in a professional and ethical manner. Within the published rules and guidelines of most professional organisations there will be specific sections covering professional ethics. If you have online access, try doing a search on the phrase 'professional ethics for accountants' to appreciate how important the topic is.

professional ethics and the AAT

In the example above the doctor will be governed by the specific standards of the medical profession in the country in which he/she practises. However, as trainee accountants you are interested in the standards that affect you in your training and when you are qualified. As a professional body the AAT has published the **Guidelines on Professional Ethics** (referred to in this text as the 'Guidelines') which have been designed to help its members maintain the high standard of professionalism that is expected of them.

The introductory page of the Guidelines emphasises the point that decisions made by members of the AAT in their professional life can have real ethical implications and that the Guidelines are designed to help members with these decisions. Specifically they state that they:

- set out the expected standard of professional behaviour
- help protect the public interest
- help to maintain the AAT's good reputation

Throughout this book we will examine in detail a number of possible areas where AAT members are faced with ethical dilemmas and we will show how the AAT Guidelines suggest that they should deal with them.

Where it is appropriate, we will refer to specific points in the AAT Guidelines. Your tutor may supply you with a copy of this document as part of your studies. It is also reproduced in Appendix 1 of this book (page 179). You can also obtain the document as a download from the AAT website (www.aat.org.uk).

to whom do the AAT Guidelines apply?

The AAT Guidelines on Professional Ethics apply to all fellow, full, affiliate and student members of the AAT. Therefore, as student members you are required to uphold the high professional standards of the AAT even before you have qualified and become a full member.

Some members of the AAT, when they become qualified, will decide to set themselves up in public practice rather than continuing to be employed. Whilst the general ethical principles within the accountancy profession will be the same for members whether they are employed or in public practice there are a number of different legal and ethical issues that are specific to each group of members.

The AAT has recognised this and has separated the Guidelines into three separate consecutive parts:

- Sections 1 to 3 cover guidance relevant to **all members**
- Section 4 provides guidance for for **employed members**
- Sections 5 to 6 is for members in **public practice**

This three-way split is shown in the diagram at the top of the next page.

organisation of the AAT Guidelines on Professional Ethics

Guidelines on
professional ethics

AAT
ASSOCIATION
OF ACCOUNTING
TECHNICIANS

Sections 1-3
relates to all AAT members

Section 4
relates to employed AAT members

Sections 5-6
relates to AAT members in public
practice

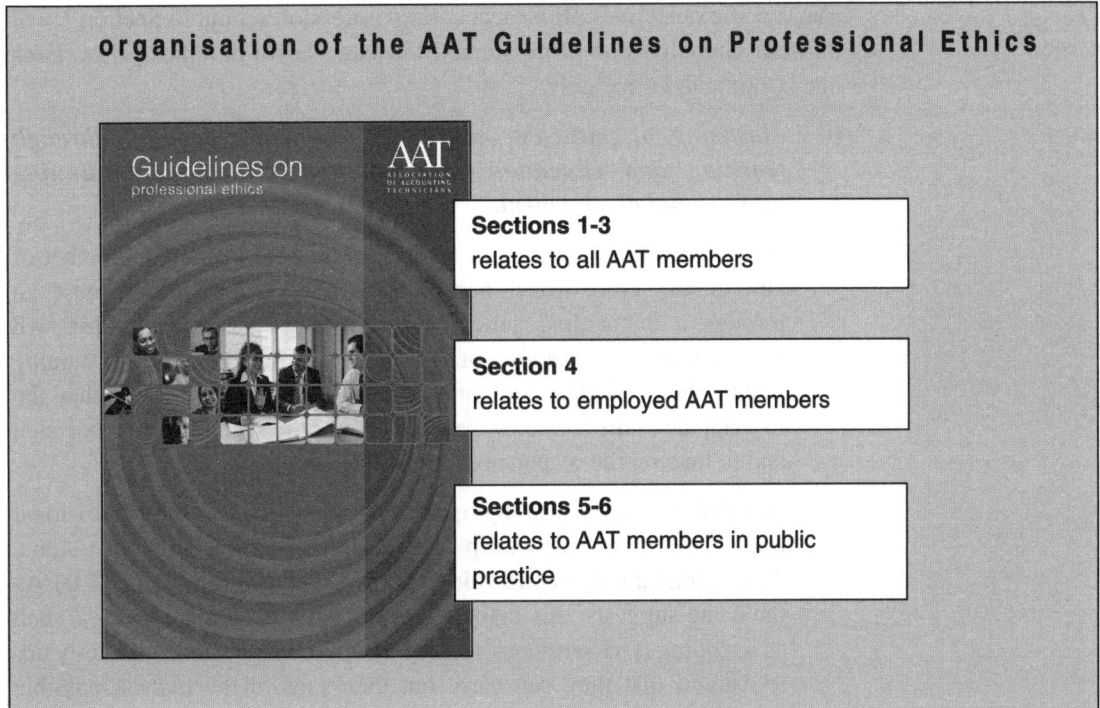

what parts of the Guidelines do you need to study?

The three-way split in the Guidelines has also been recognised in the three
elements that make up Unit 32, Professional Ethics:

■ element 32.1 covers the general principles and procedures within the
accounting section

■ element 32.2 covers issues specific to employer/employee situations

■ element 32.3 concentrates on ethics in public practice

This Unit requires that you should study all three elements and the whole of
the Guidelines document. Consequently, even if you currently work as an
employee you are still expected to have a clear understanding of professional
ethics in public practice and vice versa.

OBJECTIVES OF THE ACCOUNTING PROFESSION

So far in this chapter we have identified the people who are expected to
maintain the professional standards of the AAT with regard to professional
ethics, and have described where guidance can be obtained. We will now
move on to the objectives of the accounting profession (including the AAT).

The specific objectives of the accounting profession set out in Section 1.6 of the AAT Guidelines on Professional Ethics are shown in italics below. Each one is explained separately.

(i) *Mastering of particular skills and techniques acquired through learning and education and maintained through continuing professional development.*

As you will know from your studies, in order to become a member of any of the professional accountancy bodies, individuals must go through a demanding series of exams and assessments. This will normally involve a number of years of study linked to relevant training within the workplace, all of which is designed to ensure that the individual is fully trained to be a member of the accountancy profession and to take on the responsibilities of the role.

In addition to their training, qualified members of all the professional bodies are expected to keep their accounting knowledge up-to-date. This is done through **continuing professional development (CPD)**. As the name suggests, this involves members undertaking activities, such as attending AAT seminars, to keep their knowledge and skills fully up-to-date so that they can carry out their jobs to the highest possible standards. We will look at CPD in more detail in Chapter 2 (page 30).

An example where a member of the accounting professional requires some CPD follows:

example

the need for CPD

James Trebor is a member of the AAT and has a successful practice preparing the financial statements of various local businesses. James completed his training in 1992 and although he is competent at what he does, he is not familiar with the new International Accounting Standards (IASs). In order to ensure that the accounts he prepares for his clients comply with the new standards he has obtained copies of the IASs and has also arranged to go on an appropriate course run by the AAT.

(ii) *Development of an ethical approach to the work and to employers and clients, acquired by experience and professional supervision under training and safeguarded by a strict ethical and disciplinary code.*

When training with a professional accountancy body, the most important thing is to pass your exams and assessments and to qualify. However, throughout your training you will also be learning from your supervisors and managers. Whilst this should obviously cover the processes and procedures involved in your job it will also teach you how to approach your work in a professional manner.

Managers who are qualified accountants should 'lead by example' and should ensure that all members of their staff work to the high standards expected of a professional accountant. As part of this they should be demonstrating strong ethical values and ensuring that they maintain the standards of the profession in their work and their dealings with clients.

For example, a manager who tells junior staff that 'it's okay to add a bit extra to their travel expenses claim because everyone does it' is clearly not acting in an ethical manner and is certainly not setting a good example for his or her staff.

(iii) *Acknowledgement of duties to society as a whole in addition to the employer or the client.*

It should be clear that professional accountants have specific duties in relation to their employers and, if they are in practice, in relation to their clients. In addition to this, the accountancy profession understand that they have a duty of care to the general public. Consequently when they are carrying out their work they should always be aware of the wider picture and should consider the implications on society as a whole, as in the example which follows.

---

example

a duty to society

Whilst preparing the year-end accounts of Flexilock Plc. the accountant, John Bailey, has discovered that the company has been disposing of untreated chemical waste in a local river. John believes that this is illegal.

What should John do with the information that he has obtained?

John is in a difficult situation: he is employed by the company and does not want to risk his job. However as a professional accountant he has a duty to society as a whole, who are likely to be harmed by the actions of the company. Initially John should raise his concerns with someone more senior in the company. If no action is taken John has an obligation to society and should report this information to the relevant authorities.

(iv) *An outlook which is essentially objective, obtained by being fair minded and free from conflicts of interest.*

A person who is **objective** is someone who bases his/her opinions and decisions on real facts and is not influenced by personal beliefs or feelings. Accountants should always be objective. In addition, when they are faced with a conflict of interest, it is their duty not to let their own self-interest – or the interests of the firm that employs them – affect the professional decision that they make. The following example shows how a conflict of interest might arise.

---

example

a conflict of interest

Jill Saunders is in practice and has been the accountant for Stallone Ltd, a local firm of house builders, for a number of years. The company has two options for its next building project and the directors have asked Jill to draw up a business plan incorporating these options. The directors' preferred option involves purchasing a plot of land directly behind Jill's house and building 20 three and four bedroom houses. Currently Jill has unspoilt views from her house. There is clearly a conflict of interest here. Jill does not want the houses to be built behind her house and consequently can no longer be objective in these circumstances.

It is very important that Jill informs the directors of Stallone as soon as possible of this conflict of interest so that they are then able to make a decision as to whether they wish her to continue to prepare the business plan.

(v) *Rendering personal services to the highest standards of conduct and performance.*

This objective can be looked at in two parts. Firstly, accountants must ensure that they carry out every piece of work to the best of their ability. They should allow sufficient time to complete the work, and should never 'cut corners' or compromise on the quality of the work performed. Secondly, accountants should ensure that they have the necessary skills to perform the work being undertaken. The following example shows how this objective may be compromised:

---

example

highest standards of conduct and performance compromised

Jasmine Chang was asked to prepare the accounts for Blue Truck Ltd. The Finance Director has asked that they be made available for the board meeting in two weeks time. Jasmine agreed to this timescale; however since then two junior members of her staff have been unwell and so have been unable to work. This has meant that Jasmine has had to prepare the accounts herself in addition to her own work.

Just before the board meeting the Finance Director noticed that the accounts appeared to contain a number of errors. He pointed this out to Jasmine who explained that she had been unable to check the detail in the accounts due to the pressures on her time. She knew that she should have spoken to the Finance Director as soon as she realised that the quality of her work might be affected by the shortage of time available to her to complete the assignment.

(vi) *Achieving acceptance by the public that members provide accountancy services in accordance with these high standards and requirements.*

The accountancy profession is very focused on ensuring the highest standards from all its members. There is also the objective that accountants should be seen by members of the public to be working to achieve these high standards. In order for this to happen, the perception of the public must be that accountants are professional and trustworthy.

In recent years there have been a number of high profile cases where the standard of work that accountants have carried out has been called into question. The most famous of these is probably the collapse of the American energy company Enron. In 2002 the auditors of Enron, Arthur Andersen, were found guilty of obstruction of justice when there was evidence that they had shredded relevant documents immediately before the firm's collapse. Although this conviction was later overturned, the general public's perception of the accountancy profession was severely damaged by what they saw as highly unethical behaviour on the part of Arthur Andersen.

We can see from these six points above that the accountancy profession, including the AAT, has set a number of demanding objectives for its members to commit to. In the next section we will describe how members can ensure that they achieve these objectives wherever possible.

FUNDAMENTAL PRINCIPLES

In order to achieve the objectives of the accountancy profession that have been explained above, a professional accountant is required to comply with a number of fundamental principles. Each of these is explained below, with practical examples. It is important to realise that many of the issues regarding professional ethics cannot be looked at on their own, but should be seen collectively. Where ethical issues arise, a number of the fundamental principles may be involved in any one particular case.

These fundamental principles are set out in Section 2 of the AAT Guidelines on Professional Ethics. They can be remembered using the letters PPDCIO, which also stands for 'Professional People Drink Champagne in Offices'. They are explained in the text that follows the diagram.

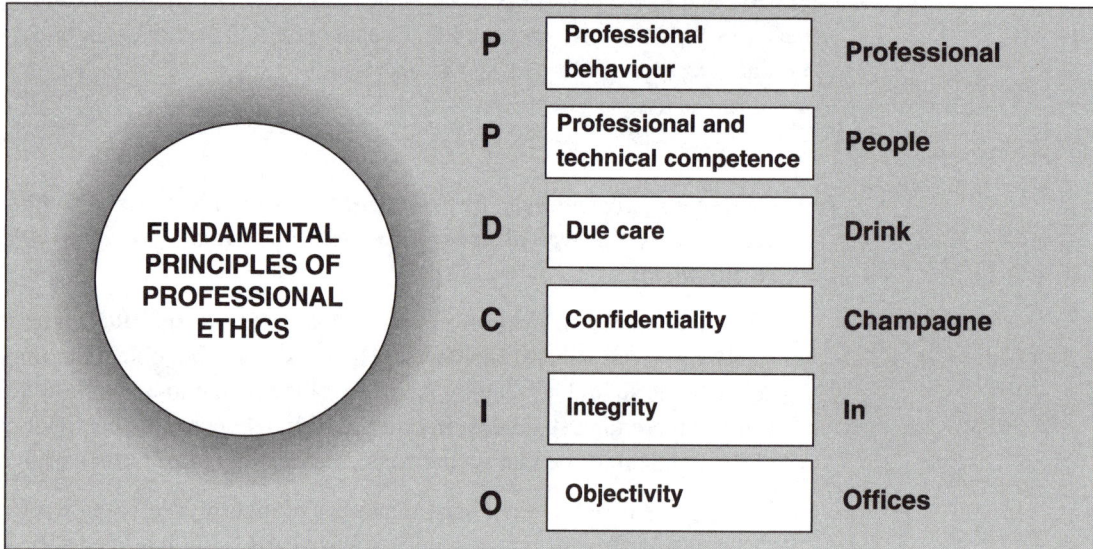

	P	Professional behaviour	**Professional**
	P	Professional and technical competence	**People**
FUNDAMENTAL PRINCIPLES OF PROFESSIONAL ETHICS	**D**	Due care	**Drink**
	C	Confidentiality	**Champagne**
	I	Integrity	**In**
	O	Objectivity	**Offices**

integrity

Section 2.1 of the AAT Guidelines states:

'Members should be straightforward and honest in performing professional work.'

Integrity is the quality of being honest and having strong moral principles that you refuse to compromise. An accountant should be straightforward and honest in performing professional work and in all business relationships.

The following situation is an example of where the integrity of an accountant might be tested.

example

a question of integrity

It is the end of the financial year and the Managing Director has told the Chief Accountant that he wants to maximise the profit for the year. He has asked the Chief Accountant not to set up a provision for doubtful debts of £60,000 against an outstanding amount that the Chief Accountant knows is unlikely to ever be paid as the customer has recently gone into liquidation.

Clearly in this situation the accountant is faced with a difficult decision. He is employed by the company and consequently has a duty to the

Managing Director. However, he knows that in order for the accounts to show the true position the debt should be provided against. In order to maintain his integrity in this situation the Chief Accountant should explain to the Managing Director that he is not prepared to ignore the bad debt and that in his opinion it should be provided for in the accounts.

objectivity

Section 2.2 of the AAT Guidelines states:

'Members should be fair and should not allow prejudice or bias or influence of others to override objectivity.'

As a professional accountant the need to remain objective at all times is very important (see also page 7). This means that any decisions that are made should be based on real facts and should not be influenced by personal beliefs or feelings. The accountant must not let his/her own bias or prejudice or pressure from others affect decisions that he/she makes.

An example where the objectivity of an accountant could be affected is illustrated in the following example.

example

a question of objectivity

Paula Gradwell is a senior accountant with a small local firm and is currently working on the year-end accounts of Bell & Sons. The owner, Alexander Bell, has asked Paula for her advice on whether the company should make a donation to the political party that he personally supports and how this will be treated in the financial statements. Paula has strong personal views against the party in question.

In this situation Paula must ensure that she remains objective when providing Alexander with advice. She must explain to him how any donation that Bell & Sons makes should be disclosed in the company's accounts. In this situation she must not let her personal opinions affect the advice that she gives.

professional and technical competence

Section 2.3.1 of the AAT Guidelines states:

'Members should refrain from undertaking or continuing any assignments which they are not competent to carry out unless advice

and assistance is obtained to ensure that the assignment is carried out satisfactorily.'

Ideally, professional accountants should only take on new assignments for which they already have the necessary professional and technical skills. However, in certain circumstances, they may take on new work for which they will need some additional help or advice, as in the following example.

example

VAT expertise

One of your firm's clients has asked you to provide specific advice on the VAT implications of a new product imported from overseas. Although you have come across VAT as part of your AAT studies it is not something with which you feel particularly comfortable. So, what options are open to you in this situation?

1   You could decline the assignment on the basis that you are not suitably competent to carry out the work involved

2   You could employ someone with the appropriate skills to complete the work you cannot do, or subcontract the parts of the assignment you are unable to undertake

3   You could arrange appropriate training for yourself to enable you to carry out the VAT work that the client has requested

In each of the three options above as a professional accountant you are ensuring that the work carried out is performed to the highest standards, either by someone else, or by you with additional training.

In Section 2.3.2 the Guidelines go further in relation to professional and technical competence. They state:

'Members also have a continuing duty:

(i)   to maintain professional knowledge and skill at a level required to ensure that a client or employer receives the advantage of competent professional service based on up-to-date developments in practice, legislation and techniques;

(ii)   to maintain their technical and ethical standards in areas relevant to their work through continuing professional development.'

This means that professional accountants have a duty to keep themselves up-to-date with developments in the accounting profession, including relevant (international) accounting or auditing standards, and also regulatory and statutory requirements. The way in which they are expected to do this is by completing continuing professional development (CPD) on a regular basis, by reading current information on technical developments in the profession or attending relevant training courses. The topic of CPD will be developed further in Chapter 2.

The influence of international accounting standards is a specific example of the need for professional accountants to update their technical knowledge through training courses run by their own professional bodies.

due care

The principle of **due care** is specifically covered in Section 2.4.1 of the Guidelines which states:

'A member, having accepted an assignment, has an obligation to carry it out with due care and reasonable despatch having regard to the nature and scope of the assignment.'

This means that when carrying out an assignment an accountant must always take the appropriate amount of care (ie '**due care**') to ensure that the quality of the work performed meets the high standards expected of the accounting profession. Each assignment must be assessed individually in relation to its importance to the client and the time allowed for its completion. Where the Guidelines refer to 'reasonable despatch' this means that the work should be completed as quickly as is reasonably possible without compromising its quality.

Section 2.4.2 then states:

'Special care is required where members undertake assignments for clients who may have little or no knowledge of accounting and taxation matters.'

This covers situations where clients are totally unfamiliar with anything to do with accounting or taxation. In such circumstances, accountants must be very careful to ensure that they carry out their work to the required standard. In addition to this they must also ensure that they explain fully to the client the results of the work that they have performed and the implications that this may have for the client.

For example, if two sole traders who do not seem to know much about accounting or taxation approach a professional accountant for financial advice as to whether they should go into partnership together, the accountant must ensure that he/she makes make each of them fully aware of all the taxation and accounting implications involved.

confidentiality

At the start of the chapter we introduced the example of a doctor who broke his patient's confidentiality by passing information to the press. All professions need to maintain confidentiality of client information. Accountants accumulate a large amount of information about their clients' affairs in the course of their work. Only in the most serious of circumstances, where there is a legal duty to disclose, would accountants be justified in revealing confidential information about their clients.

Section 2.5 of the Guidelines states:

'Members should respect the confidentiality of information acquired during the course of performing professional work and should not use or disclose any such information without proper and specific authority or unless there is a legal or professional right or duty to disclose.'

The example below raises the issue of confidentiality.

---

example

a question of confidentiality

You work for an accounting practice with a large number of clients in the local area. One Friday evening you have dinner with a good friend who explains that he has been offered a job with a local firm of publishers. He knows that they are one of your firm's clients and over dinner he asks you what their financial position is like and whether you feel that it would be a good move for him.

How should you deal with his questions?

In order to maintain the confidentiality of your client you should not disclose any information that is not already in the public domain. You should explain the need for confidentiality to your friend. You could suggest that he get the latest set of published accounts from Companies House which would give him an idea of the financial position of the company.

The subject of confidentiality and examples of situations when it can be broken are covered in detail in Chapter 3 (pages 35 - 42).

professional behaviour

The final fundamental principle detailed in Section 2 of the Guidelines on Professional Ethics is that of professional behaviour. Section 2.6 states:

'Members should act in a manner consistent with the good reputation of the profession and refrain from any conduct which might bring discredit to the profession.'

As we have seen earlier in this chapter the accountancy profession is respected for the high standards that it requires of its members. Therefore, members must always ensure that they do not bring the profession into disrepute by acting in any way which is unprofessional or does not comply with relevant laws and regulations.

For example, a member of the AAT who sends offensive or inappropriate emails from their place of work would be considered unprofessional. In addition this could reflect very badly on the firm that he works for and also on the AAT.

A much more serious example of a member damaging the reputation of the accountancy profession would be if he or she gave professional advice to a client that the member knew failed to comply with relevant laws and regulations.

Chapter Summary

■ Members of all professional accounting bodies should maintain the standards of that organisation.

■ The professional ethics of an organisation are the moral principles or standards that govern the conduct of its members.

■ The Guidelines on Professional Ethics issued by the AAT give its members guidance in situations where ethical conflicts arise.

■ The Guidelines on Professional Ethics document is split into three sections:
- general principles, applicable to all members
- guidance specifically for employed members
- guidance for members in practice

■ The Guidelines state that the accountancy profession (including the AAT) is committed to six objectives:
- mastering skills and techniques through learning and training
- developing an ethical approach to work and observing a code of ethics
- acknowledging a duty to society as a whole
- adopting an objective approach, free from conflicts of interest
- providing accounting services to the highest standards
- ensuring that the public knows that accountants provide services to these high standards

■ In order to achieve these objectives all members should observe the fundamental principles set out in Section 2 of the Guidelines, listed below.

■ The Guidance sets out six fundamental principles:
- integrity
- objectivity
- professional and technical competence
- due care
- confidentiality
- professional behaviour

Key Terms	**professional ethics**	the moral principles or standards that govern the conduct of the members of an organisation
	Guidelines on Professional Ethics	A document issued by the AAT providing guidance to full and student members regarding professional ethics
	integrity	members should be straightforward and honest in performing professional duties
	continuing professional development	members of professional accounting bodies are expected to keep their technical knowledge up-to-date through relevant study, training and by attending courses
	objectivity	decisions should be made based on true facts and accountants must not let their own bias or prejudice, or pressure from others affect decisions that they make
	conflict of interest	these arise where the business or personal interests of a member may intervene to prevent the member giving an objective opinion
	professional and technical competence	members have a duty to ensure that they have the necessary skills to carry out any work that is assigned to them
	due care	accountants must always take sufficient care to ensure that the quality of their work meets the high standards expected of them
	confidentiality	information obtained during the course of professional work should not be disclosed without proper and specific authority or unless there is a legal duty to do so
	professional behaviour	accountants should maintain the good reputation of the profession and should not do anything to discredit the profession

Student Activities

answers to the asterisked (*) questions are to be found at the back of this book.

You work for G Verdi & Co., a small firm of accountants in Oak Town. G Verdi & Co has a number of clients in the area. During the week a number of situations arise which involve ethical issues.

1.1*   You are out for dinner in a local restaurant with a friend when you notice that one of the partners in a local firm of solicitors which is a client of yours is sitting at a table nearby. You do not recognise the person with him but know that it isn't his wife or his business partner. As he is making no attempt to lower his voice you hear some of his conversation. He is explaining some confidential information about a number of his clients to his companion and is also saying that he is seriously considering leaving the partnership and setting up on his own.

Explain the ethical issues for you that are raised by this situation and whether you need to take any action.

1.2*   A member of your firm's staff has submitted his expense claim to you for approval. When you review the form you notice that he has claimed that it was 20 miles to Brown & Co.'s premises. You have visited them yourself and know the journey is only 14 miles. For a second client he has claimed travel expenses for a week, but you are almost certain that he has been given a lift by another member of staff from your firm who was also working on the assignment.

Should you approve the expense claim? What ethical issues does this raise?

1.3*   A local car dealership has asked your firm to provide a training course for its accounting staff entitled 'Credit Control without Tears.' Although you have staff with the necessary technical skills, none of the staff has ever done any training and they are nervous about carrying out this task.

Should you accept the assignment? Justify your decision.

1.4   It is the end of the tax year and a large number of your clients require their accounts to be completed and their tax returns to be prepared. A large potential client has approached your firm with a project which they have stressed needs to be completed 'as soon as possible.' All of your staff are stretched with their existing workload.

Would it be ethically correct for your firm you accept this assignment? Explain the fundamental principles that would be relevant in these circumstances?

1.5   Your firm is considering extending their current premises and, having gained the necessary planning permission, they have approached three local builders. The following are comments received from these three firms:

■   'We'll do some of the work for cash, that way you can avoid VAT and we can leave it out of our accounts.'

■   'Tell us what everyone else quotes and we guarantee to charge you 15% less.'

■   'Maybe we could come to some sort of arrangement where you do our accounts and we charge you less than full price for the work.'

Explain the ethical issues raised by these comments that would influence the decision of your firm whether to employ any of these builders to carry out the extension work you have planned.

Objectivity and professional competence

This chapter explains the practical approach that the AAT takes to professional ethics and looks in more detail at objectivity and the need for an accountant to be independent. The chapter also deals with the way in which ethical problems can be resolved and finally covers the ways in which accountants ensure that they are sufficiently competent to carry out their work.

Specific areas covered include:

■ *the difference between a principle and a rule-based approach to professional ethics*

■ *the principles of objectivity and independence*

■ *how to resolve ethical conflict*

■ *presentation of information*

■ *attaining and maintaining professional competence*

PERFORMANCE CRITERIA COVERED

unit 32: PROFESSIONAL ETHICS

Element 32.1:

apply general principles and procedures for ethical compliance expected within the accounting sector

A   *Identify and apply fundamental principles of honesty and integrity.*

B   *Highlight situations within professional work that require objectivity and fairness, and where judgements and actions could compromise personal or organisational integrity and reputation.*

C   *Recognise the principles of effective Continuing Professional Development (CPD) to maintain professional and technical competence (to include sources of advice and information outside formal learning).*

F   *Identify the key issues which ensure professional services are performed within the scope of professional ethics guidance.*

G   *Make critical decisions to identify appropriate ethical behaviour when interfacing with others in a variety of circumstances.*

H   *Refer and seek advice from relevant sources for issues beyond own <u>professional</u> competence.*

J   *Discuss, agree and resolve any ethical conflict.*

A PRINCIPLE-BASED APPROACH

what are the principles?

Chapter 1 of this book covered the fundamental principles of professional ethics. You may remember the mnemonic: **P**rofessional **P**eople **D**rink **C**hampagne **I**n **O**ffices. This will remind you of the six fundamental principles of professional ethics:

- Professional and Technical Competence
- Professional Behaviour
- Due Care
- Confidentiality
- Integrity
- Objectivity

The AAT believes that its members should take a principle-based approach to professional ethics. This means that when faced with ethical decisions members should consider their decisions based on these fundamental principles rather than using a rigid system of rules and regulations.

We have seen that these principles are general in nature and so cannot be applied rigidly in specific situations to solve ethical problems that members come across in their working lives. When ethical dilemmas occur these principles should be considered together with the **Guidelines on Professional Ethics** ('Guidelines') produced by the AAT. Members should use their judgement and make all necessary enquiries before any decision is reached on ethical matters.

principle-based approach v rule-based approach

The AAT makes the comparison between a principle-based approach and a rule-based approach as follows:

'A principle-based approach means that you look at the objective that is to be achieved and focus on that objective.'

'A rule-based approach means that you apply the rules exactly as stated regardless of the circumstances (ie literally).'

What the AAT is saying here is that its preferred approach, where possible, is that members should look at the objective to be achieved and focus on that objective rather than sticking rigidly to a set of rules.

The difference between a principle-based approach and a rule-based approach can be seen in the example that now follows.

---

example

principle-based approach v rule-based approach

Your firm of accountants has recently been taken on to provide professional accounting services for James Roberts, who is a self-employed painter and decorator. When preparing James's end of year accounts you realise that, early on in the year, the business's turnover has exceeded the annual limit for Valued Added Tax (VAT). This means that James should have registered for VAT and should from that point have been charging VAT on his services.

What should you do in this situation?

Taking a rule-based approach you would report James to HMRC for failing to register for VAT when his business had reached the VAT limit. This would arguably be a harsh course of action.

The preferred principle-based approach, on the other hand, would involve explaining to James that he must register for VAT immediately and should also make Her Majesty's Revenue and Customs (HMRC) aware of the delay in registering that has occurred and the fact that he has not charged VAT on his services during the year as he should have done. Using this approach, you have identified the main issue – which is that James registers for VAT as soon as possible – and you have given James the necessary professional advice to allow him to do so.

OBJECTIVITY

what is objectivity?

One of the fundamental principles covered in Chapter 1 is **objectivity**. In Section 2.2 of the Guidelines, the AAT emphasises the need for all of its members to maintain objectivity at all times. A person who is objective has already been defined in Chapter 1 as someone who bases his/her opinions and decisions on real facts and is not influenced by personal beliefs or feelings or those of other people. It is also important for an accountant to ensure that he/she collects all the information that is required before making any judgements.

The Guidelines then go on to look at objectivity in more detail in Section 3.1.1 where it says that there is:

'an obligation on all members to be fair-minded, intellectually honest and free from conflicts of interest.'

'Fair-minded' means that an accountant should treat every situation equally and ensure that every point of view is given equal consideration. Intellectual honesty means the accountant should gather, analyse and present information accurately. The fact that all members need to be free from conflicts of interest means that they must not allow their own self-interest or that of the organisation that they work for to influence any decision that they make.

independence

The principle of objectivity goes hand-in-hand with the need for independence. A definition of independence is **'freedom from control or influence of others'**.

An accountant must always carry out his/her work in an independent way and regardless of any external pressure. There may be people who try and put pressure on an accountant, or even make threats to try to ensure that the accountant's work is performed to best suit their needs. In order to act in a professional and ethical manner the accountant must not be influenced by this pressure and must remain independent.

example

a question of independence

Amerdeep Johal works for a firm of accountants and is currently preparing the year-end accounts for ABP Supplies, a local company owned by two brothers Andrew and Brian Potter. Amerdeep has calculated a draft profit figure for the year of £56,000 compared with £127,000 in the previous year. During a meeting with the two brothers Andrew says that he is not happy with this profit figure as he has a meeting with the bank at the end of the week to discuss a loan and he knows they will be unhappy with such a large drop in profit. He asks Amerdeep if there is any way that he could 'improve' the profit figure.

Amerdeep explains that this would not be appropriate as the accounts would no longer give an accurate picture of the financial state of affairs of the business. Andrew replies that he will need to speak to the partner in the firm that Amerdeep works for who is a close friend of his and if this is not resolved he may consider changing the firm of accountants that ABP Supplies uses.

In this situation Amerdeep is being pressured by Andrew. Firstly, he will feel personal pressure as Andrew has threatened to speak to Amerdeep's boss. Secondly, he has threatened to take his business elsewhere which will have an impact on the firm that Amerdeep works for. In order to remain independent Amerdeep should not allow these pressures to influence him. He must stick to his principles and, provided his boss has the same ethical principles, Amerdeep should be confident that he will support him and will not expect Amerdeep to change his opinion.

In stressing the importance for members of the AAT to remain independent, the Guidelines state that members must be both **independent of mind** and **independent in appearance**. We will now describe what is meant by these.

independence of mind

The Guidelines, Section 3.1.4 (ii) give the following definition of independence of mind:

'the state of mind which has regard to all considerations relevant to the tasks in hand but no other – independence of mind is also referred to as objectivity'

What this means is that when carrying out work and making decisions, a professional accountant should only take into account points and issues which are relevant to the job that he or she is doing. As the definition states, this is more or less the same as the principle of objectivity which we have discussed above.

independence in appearance

First we will consider the definition given in the Guidelines, Section 3.1.4 (ii):

'the avoidance of situations inducing so obvious a threat to independence that an informed third party would question the member's objectivity'.

In addition to maintaining objectivity and independence, an accountant must ensure that he or she is **seen to be** independent. This means that anyone who comes into contact with the accountant must be confident that he/she always behaves independently and has avoided doing anything that may bring that independence into question.

The following example highlights a situation that may affect the **independence in appearance** of a professional accountant.

example

independence in appearance

Ashton and Groves is a small firm of accountants in Broom Town. One of the partners, Jemima Ashton, is married to Frank, who owns a local car dealership, Ashton Motors. For many years Ashton Motors have used Edwards & Co, another firm of accountants in the town, to prepare their year-end accounts. But Jim Edwards has just retired and Edwards & Co have ceased to operate.

Frank has suggested that the obvious solution would be for Ashton and Groves to take on the preparation of Ashton Motors accounts. But would this be appropriate?

The answer is no. Jemima, one of the Ashton & Groves partners, is clearly linked to the car dealership because she is married to Frank, its owner. Even if she had no involvement in the preparation of the accounts for Ashton Motors, her close personal relationship with Frank means that any outsider could quite justifiably question the independence and objectivity of Ashton and Groves.

safeguarding independence and objectivity

There are a number of factors that will influence an accountant and safeguard his/her independence and objectivity.

- Throughout their training professional accountants have been taught to act in a professional and ethical manner. They will be able to identify situations that could potentially affect their independence and they will be able to deal effectively with threats or pressures exerted on them.

- An accountant should be aware of the possibility of legal action if he/she gives in to pressures that are exerted and allows his/her independence to be compromised.

- Members of any one of the professional accounting bodies such as AAT, CIMA or ACCA, are aware of the possibility of professional disciplinary procedures against them from these bodies if they do not remain independent at all times.

- Finally, if an accountant is found to have compromised his/her objectivity and independence, this could potentially damage the accountant's reputation. The loss of professional reputation will often lead to the loss of clients and ultimately to loss of earnings.

acceptance of gifts

One possible threat to the independence of an accountant which is highlighted in the Guidelines (Section 3.1.5) is the acceptance of gifts, services, favours or hospitality from a client. This is because there is a risk that these gifts could influence the work performed and decisions made by the accountant, effectively by bribing the accountant.

The problem here is whether all gifts should be refused or whether it is acceptable to receive certain small gifts and favours. There is an argument that accepting a bottle of wine or some chocolates from a client at Christmas will not influence an accountant's work or opinions. However, would this still be the case if the gift was a case of wine? At what point would it no longer be appropriate to accept such gifts?

The following example illustrates this issue.

---

example

Merry Christmas!

Simon Fuller works for Adams & Co, a firm of accountants in Bridgetown. During the week before Christmas, Sara, one of the owners of Peroni, a local restaurant which is one of the firm's clients, turns up at the office with a crate of champagne. Sara hands it to Simon together with a Christmas card and wishes him a Happy Christmas. She suggests that he gives a bottle to each member of staff. Sara says 'tell Roger Adams that I've arranged the table for your firm's Christmas party on Friday and not to worry about the bill as it's on Peroni!'

What are the ethical implications of this situation? Should Simon Fuller accept the champagne and should Adams & Co accept the offer of a free Christmas meal from Peroni?

With regard to the champagne it is unlikely that if each member of staff accepts a bottle of champagne this will influence their independence when working on the accounts of Peroni. The acceptance of a free Christmas meal, however, is another matter. This is likely to mean a substantial cost saving for Adams & Co. If a third party was aware of this they may consider that Adams & Co could be influenced by the financial benefit that they are getting by not paying for the meal. Even if the owners of Peroni say that they do not expect anything in return, Adams & Co should decline the offer, enjoy the meal and ensure that they pay for it in full.

From this example it can be seen that there are no rules regarding what is and what is not acceptable. A professional accountant must use professional judgement and experience to decide whether he or she is allowed to accept gifts from a client. In most cases, however, if there is any question in the accountant's mind he or she should politely refuse a gift from a client.

PRESENTATION OF INFORMATION

The need for clear presentation of financial information is covered in Section 3.2 of the Guidelines, which emphasises that the AAT expects its members to present financial information 'fully, honestly and professionally and so that it will be understood in its context'. This means that they should disclose all relevant figures and supporting documentation without bias and in a way that the reader can understand clearly.

The Guidelines then go on to say that 'financial information should describe clearly the true nature of business transactions, assets and liabilities.'

This section of the Guidelines highlights the importance for members of the AAT to ensure that when they prepare financial information they remember the needs of the users and always ensure that the information that they present is a true reflection of the financial state of affairs of the business.

In addition to this, accountants must prepare this information in accordance with accepted accounting standards.

The example that follows demonstrates the need for clear presentation of financial information.

example

the value of chocolate

You are assistant accountant for Top Chocs, a company which supplies quality boxes of chocolates to retail stores. It is the end of February and you have been included in the team to perform the annual stock count for the year ended 28 February. This involves counting all the stock that is held on the company's premises, checking it to the stock records and placing an accurate value on it.

During the stock count you discover 20 crates which each contain 500 boxes of Christmas chocolates. When you check the stock records you find that these chocolates are still being valued at the full cost. By the time next Christmas comes these chocolates will no longer be edible and are realistically now only fit to be sold at a heavily discounted price.

In order to ensure that the accounts give a true picture of the state of the company's financial affairs these items of stock must be valued in accordance with the appropriate accounting standards – in this case SSAP 9, 'Stock and work in progress' or the international equivalent IAS 2 'Inventories'. These both state that stock should be valued at the lower of cost and net realisable value. Therefore the stock must be written down in the financial statements to whatever value it can be sold for.

RESOLUTION OF ETHICAL CONFLICTS

This book aims to explain how professional ethics affect the working lives of members of the accountancy profession. In order to illustrate this, many of the examples that have been used throughout this book involve situations where the accountant is faced with an ethical conflict. Some of the issues may be relatively minor. In some cases, however, an accountant may be faced with more serious matters such as fraud or other illegal activities.

The Guidelines give specific guidance on how to deal with ethical conflict in a number of cases which are detailed below. The number quoted in each case relates to the Section of the Guidelines and the words in italics are taken from the Guidelines. Each point is explained separately and illustrated with a brief example.

3.3.1 *If members are instructed or encouraged to engage in any activity which is unlawful they are entitled and required to decline. For example, members should not be party to the falsification of any record or knowingly or recklessly supply any information or make any statement which is misleading, false or deceptive.*

This means that a member should not under any circumstances do anything that is illegal. If a client or colleague asks or tells them to do something that is against the law, false or dishonest they must refuse.

example

making bread – a question of pay

You have recently been offered the job as the accountant for Frankley and Peters, a local firm that runs a small chain of bakeries. Part of your duties is to prepare the payroll for all staff. Janet Peters tells you that the company pays all their staff a basic wage on which PAYE and National Insurance Contributions (NICs) are paid – the remainder is paid in cash.

What should you do?

This practice is illegal as all earnings should be taken into account when calculating and paying PAYE and NICs. Consequently you should tell Janet that you are not prepared to carry on with this practice and that you will not be able to accept the position unless all wages are correctly accounted for by the business.

3.3.2 *If the member would feel uncomfortable defending an action in open court or to the press then it is likely that such a course of action should be avoided on ethical grounds.*

The point here is that if an accountant is faced with a situation that he/she is unsure of, the accountant must decide whether he/she would be prepared to go to court and defend the action that he/she takes. If there is any doubt in the accountant's mind he/she should avoid the action in question.

example

client list confidentiality

You work for a small firm of accountants which has recently taken on a new member of staff. She explains that she is still in touch with some of her old colleagues from her previous place of work and could easily get you a copy of their client list. This would then in her words 'give you a readymade list of potential new clients to approach, especially as I know what these clients are currently paying their accountants.'

Would it be appropriate to accept this offer?

This is a clear breach of confidentiality on the part of your new employee. Approaching these clients on this basis is not acceptable and could result in the other firm taking legal action against your firm. In this situation you should explain to the new member of staff that this is extremely unethical and cannot be considered in any circumstances.

3.3.3 *An honest difference of opinion between a member and another person is not itself an ethical issue.*

If an accountant disagrees with a client or colleague this is not necessarily an ethical conflict, provided the disagreement is an honest one and the viewpoint of each side is valid. It becomes an ethical conflict when the accountant believes that the opinion or action of the client or colleague is unethical or unlawful.

example

a question of value

You work as the Financial Accountant for Snax, a biscuit manufacturer. It is the end of the financial year and you and the Financial Controller are discussing the valuation of year end stock. The Financial Controller believes that stock should be valued at the average cost (AVCO) whereas you prefer the more prudent approach of valuing stock using First in Fist out (FIFO).

Is there an ethical issue in this situation?

Under Standard Statement of Accounting Practice 9 (and IAS 2) both AVCO and FIFO are acceptable methods of valuing stock. Therefore, whilst there is clearly a difference of opinion between you and the Financial Controller, there is no question that any action taken by the Financial Controller would be unethical or unlawful.

3.3.4 *In resolving ethical conflicts the member should consider seeking counselling and advice on a confidential basis with an independent legal advisor and/or the Ethics Advice Line.*

This highlights the point that a professional accountant should know when to ask for advice. When AAT members come up against a potential ethical problem that they do not feel confident dealing with they should either take legal advice or they should contact the AAT Ethics Advice Line.

example

finding a fraud – taking advice

Your boss is away on holiday and you have been asked to cover his job for the next two weeks. Whilst carrying out his job it becomes apparent to you that he has been making unauthorised payments from the company bank account into his own personal account without any supporting documentation.

What should you do in this situation?

Your immediate reaction would probably be to report him to his manager. However, there is always the risk that his manager could also be involved in the potential fraud. It may be more appropriate in this situation to seek advice from a third party. This could be from a solicitor or from the AAT Ethics Advice Line. It is quite likely that the advice they give will be to report the matter to the senior management of the business, but it is always worth seeking advice if you are unsure in a situation such as this.

3.3.5 *It is important to keep a written record of all meetings and discussions which take place in seeking to resolve ethical conflict.*

When a member of the AAT is faced with an ethical conflict it is very important to make sure that he/she keeps a note of all meetings and discussions that are held to try and resolve the conflict. This will include details of who attended the meeting, what was discussed and any decisions that were reached. One of the main reasons for this is that this will act as proof if ever the accountant is faced with legal proceedings.

example

finding a fraud – keeping records

Consider again the example shown above ('finding a fraud – taking advice') where your boss has been found to be defrauding the company. In this situation you must always ensure that you keep a written record of discussions you have had with solicitors or the AAT Ethics Advice Line as proof that you have taken steps to resolve the ethical conflict with which you have been faced. If and when you report the matter to senior management within your organisation you must also ensure that all meetings and discussions are accurately recorded.

In Section 3.3.6 the Guidelines also link the issue of ethical conflict to 'Conflict of loyalties' which will be covered in Chapter 4 (for employed members) and Chapter 5 (for members in practice).

The key issues that have emerged over the last few pages are that members of the accounting profession should never do anything that they believe to be illegal or unethical; where they are faced with an ethical conflict that they cannot resolve they should seek advice from a solicitor or from the AAT Ethics Advice Line.

PROFESSIONAL COMPETENCE

Before taking on a new client or a new piece of work, an accountant must make sure that he/she has the ability to carry out the work involved and the necessary professional competence to complete the job. This is specifically covered in Section 3.4.1 of the Guidelines which states:

'Members should refrain from undertaking or continuing assignments which they are not competent to carry out unless competent advice and assistance is obtained to enable them to satisfactorily carry out the assignment.'

There are two separate issues which relate to a member's competence. First of all, a member must gain (attain) professional competence. Secondly, a member must ensure that he/she maintains professional competence. We will now explain each of these in turn.

attainment of professional competence

Most people who are reading this book will be studying to become a member of the AAT and will probably be working in an accounting related job. By the time all the training, assessment and examinations have been successfully completed to allow a person to become a member of the AAT this should mean that they have gained the necessary professional competence.

maintenance of professional competence

This is not, however, the end of the training for a professional accountant. Regardless of the professional body which has awarded the qualification, there is a requirement to maintain a level of professional competence. Members must keep up-to-date with all new developments in the accounting profession: as you know from your studies in other units accounting standards are changing both nationally and internationally. Accountants are required to keep up-to-date with all these changes, together with any other relevant amendments to auditing standards or other legislation such as changes in taxation laws.

The preferred way for members of the AAT to maintain professional competence is through **continued professional development** (CPD). This is learning that accountants need to carry out to stay competent so that they are effective and successful throughout their chosen career.

The AAT Council recommends that its members should follow a programme of relevant continuing professional development (CPD) of at least 60 hours over a period of two years with at least 20 hours in any single year. The following are specific examples of appropriate CPD that have been identified by the AAT:

- workshops, training courses, conferences

- AAT or other professional body branch/society meetings

- planned coaching from colleagues or specialists

- structured discussion groups

- studying for further qualifications

- on-line/CD-Rom courses

- planned reading/research

- using audio, video or IT resources

- special project work or job secondment

- hands-on development of skills (eg IT or presentations)

- membership of local or professional groups

- voluntary work

With all the choices above, it would seem very straightforward for an accountant to achieve the required amount of CPD. However, it is very important to stress that the CPD that is undertaken by the accountant must be relevant, and significant learning must take place. For example attending a local AAT meeting is only relevant CPD if the subjects discussed are relevant to the accountant's job. Similarly, acting voluntarily as treasurer for a local cricket club may be relevant CPD but working on a Saturday morning as a dog walker at the local dog shelter may not be!

Chapter Summary

- When ethical decisions need to be taken, a principle-based approach should be adopted, based on the objective to be achieved rather than applying the rules exactly as stated.

- Accountants must follow the principle of objectivity which is key to professional accountants remaining independent.

- When making decisions, an accountant must ensure that he/she remains independent of mind and only take into account issues and points that are relevant to the issues that they are addressing.

- In addition to independence of mind, the accountant must demonstrate independence in appearance. This means that they should avoid situations that could make a third party question the accountant's objectivity.

- A professional accountant must use his or her professional judgement to decide whether to accept gifts from a client.

- When an accountant prepares financial information it should be presented fully, honestly and professionally and should clearly describe the true nature of business transactions, assets and liabilities.

- Where ethical conflicts arise, accountants should take all necessary steps to resolve these, and if necessary should seek advice from a solicitor or from the AAT Ethics Advice Line.

- Members of the AAT and other professional accountants should only accept new work if they are professionally competent to carry it out.

- A member attains professional competence through training and qualifying as an accountant.

- To maintain professional competence members of the AAT and other professional accounting bodies should undertake a programme of continuing professional development.

<table>
<tr><td rowspan="8">

Key Terms

</td><td>

principle-based approach

</td><td>the approach to professional ethics that means you look at the objective that is to be achieved and focus on that objective</td></tr>
<tr><td>

rule-based approach

</td><td>the approach to professional ethics that means that you apply any rules exactly as stated regardless of the circumstances</td></tr>
<tr><td>

objectivity

</td><td>not allowing personal beliefs or feelings or pressure from others to affect decisions that are made</td></tr>
<tr><td>

independence of mind

</td><td>only taking into account points that are relevant to decisions to be made or work that is being undertaken – this is very similar to objectivity</td></tr>
<tr><td>

independence in appearance

</td><td>ensuring that to a third party the actions taken by the accountant appear to be objective and free from the influence of others</td></tr>
<tr><td>

ethical conflict

</td><td>this occurs where there is a fundamental disagreement between what has been requested of the accountant and what his/her ethical principles indicate that he/she should do</td></tr>
<tr><td>

professional competence

</td><td>the necessary skills and expertise to carry out existing or new assignments to the required standards</td></tr>
<tr><td>

continuing professional development (CPD)

</td><td>members of professional accounting bodies are expected to keep their technical knowledge up-to-date through relevant study and training, and by attending appropriate courses</td></tr>
</table>

Student Activities

answers to the asterisked (*) questions are to be found at the back of this book.

You are a senior manager at Henderson and Brighton a firm of accountants based in Chesterridge. During one week in January the following situations arise:

2.1 *   A potential client arrives at the office on Monday morning to attend a meeting with you to discuss his tax situation. He explains that he has been working as a self-employed plumber for the last four years and has managed to maintain a comfortable standard of living from the profits he has made. To-date he has never filled in a tax return and consequently has never paid any tax on his profits. He is considering employing Henderson and Brighton to prepare his future tax returns and has yet to decide what to do about the tax returns for previous years.

Based on estimates of his profit for the last four years it would appear that his tax liability for these years is likely to be substantial. Explain what action you might take if you follow:

(a) a principle-based approach

(b) a rule-based approach

2.2 *   One of your responsibilities as a senior manager at Henderson and Brighton is for the recruitment of new staff. The firm is currently looking to employ a new manager and you have a second interview booked with a possible candidate, Nisha Patel, on Tuesday afternoon. The interview is going very well and during discussions with Nisha she reveals that her father owns a large catering business which is one of Henderson and Brighton's biggest clients.

In view of this information, explain whether it is appropriate for your firm to employ Nisha. What ethical issues are raised by this situation and what steps could be taken if she is taken on?

2.3*   When you arrive at work on Wednesday morning there is a letter on your desk from one of your clients, Far To Go, which operates a travel agency in Chesterridge. In the letter the owner says that he is offering 40% discount to all members of staff at Henderson and Brighton if they book their holiday with Far To Go. You know that this is the same discount that Far To Go offer their own staff.

Would it be appropriate to accept this offer from Far To Go? Explain the reasons for your decision?

2.4   Amanda Blight is the owner of Cut and Blow, a hair salon in Chesterridge, which has been a client of Henderson and Brighton for several years. She arrives at your office on Thursday afternoon with all the business's financial records for you to prepare the accounts for Cut and Blow for the year ended 30 November 2005.

She explains that she has been considering selling the business for a while and has found a buyer who appears to be keen. She has already told the potential buyer that the profit for the year is likely to be close to £110,000 although she now knows that the actual profit is likely to be nearer £75,000. She has asked you to include some of the sales for December 2005 in the previous year and to leave out some of the expenses that were incurred at the end of the financial year.

Should you agree to do what Amanda is asking? Explain the reasons for your decision.

2.5   You are due to give a brief presentation on Friday morning to the rest of the staff of Henderson and Brighton on Continuing Professional Development (CPD). Make appropriate notes on:

- the purpose of CPD and why it is important
- what the AAT requires from members regarding CPD
- what sort of things are appropriate evidence of CPD

3 Confidentiality and taxation services

this chapter covers . . .

This chapter looks in more detail at the principle of confidentiality in relation to professional ethics and describes the ethical points relating to taxation work carried out by an accountant for a client or employer.

Specific areas covered include:

■ *the accountant's duty of confidentiality in relation to the client's or employer's affairs*

■ *the circumstances where confidential information can be disclosed*

■ *ethical points relating to taxation services such as tax computations, completion of tax returns and giving of tax advice*

PERFORMANCE CRITERIA COVERED

unit 32: PROFESSIONAL ETHICS

Element 32.1:

apply general principles and procedures for ethical compliance expected within the accounting sector

A   Identify and apply fundamental principles of honesty and integrity.

B   Highlight situations within professional work that require objectivity and fairness and where judgements and actions could compromise personal or organisational integrity and reputation.

D   Recognise and explain why certain types of information should be regarded as confidential.

E   Identify circumstances when it would be appropriate to disclose confidential information.

F   Identify the key issues which ensure professional services are performed within the scope of professional ethics guidance.

G   Make critical decisions to identify appropriate ethical behaviour when interacting with others in a variety of circumstances.

H   Refer and seek advice from relevant sources for issues beyond own <u>professional competence</u>.

I   *Describe the types of contractual obligations you would have in providing services to clients to include due care and carrying out assignments within a reasonable timescale.*

J   *Discuss, agree and resolve any ethical conflict.*

CONFIDENTIALITY

duty of confidentiality

One of the principles of professional ethics that we first introduced in Chapter 1 is **confidentiality**. This means that information obtained during the course of an accountant's professional work should not be disclosed without proper and specific authority or unless there is a legal duty to do so. As this is such a fundamental principle of professional ethics, the Guidelines go into detail on confidentiality in section 3.5.

Members of the AAT have a 'duty of confidentiality' which means that they have **an obligation to respect the confidentiality of information about a client's or employer's affairs which has been gained during their employment or during the course of their professional work**. In addition to ensuring that they themselves observe this duty of confidentiality members must also make sure that any staff they supervise or manage also respect the principle of confidentiality.

We now give an example of a situation where a member must observe his/her duty of confidentiality.

example

a duty of confidentiality

Elliot Graves has been employed in the accounts department of Simons & Simons for a number of years and currently works as the Financial Accountant for the firm. On the train home from work on Friday evening he meets a friend and they start chatting. The conversation moves on to work and his friend asks Elliot how the job is going. He then goes on to ask how Simons & Simons are doing and specifically asks what kind of a financial year the company has had.

How should Elliot answer his friend's questions?

Elliot has a duty of confidentiality to his employers not to disclose any confidential information about the company that he works for. Elliot can answer his friend's first question as to whether his job is going well as this is a personal enquiry about Elliot himself. However, Elliot should explain to his friend that it is not appropriate for him to discuss confidential information about Simons & Simons financial results.

using confidential information

In addition to ensuring that they do not disclose confidential information, members of the AAT must ensure that they do not use, or appear to use, any information that they have access to for their own personal advantage or for the advantage of a third party.

We will now look in more detail at what this actually means. The point is illustrated in the following example.

example

a question of advice

Lubna Mirza is employed by a small firm of accountants and has been working on the year-end accounts of one of their largest clients, Richards Ltd. During the time that she spends at the client's premises Lubna learns that the company is currently in talks to take over another local company which is owned by a close friend of hers. The owner of Richards Ltd, James Richards, has mentioned that he would be willing to pay up to £250,000 for the firm, but only initially intends to offer £200,000.

Should Lubna tell her friend about James Richards' intentions? If not, would it be acceptable for her to give her friend advice about what offer to accept for her business?

Lubna has a duty of confidentiality to the client and so should not disclose any information she has obtained about Richards Ltd without specific authority from the company or unless she is legally obliged to do so. If she were to give her friend advice about what offer to accept, based on the information that she now knows, she would be using information that she had gained to benefit her friend (a third party), which is not acceptable.

Therefore, if Lubna's friend asks her for advice she should explain that Richards Ltd is one of her firm's clients and should suggest that the friend obtains independent specialist advice how to value her business.

This example shows that an accountant must not use information for his/her personal advantage or for that of a third party.

We will now look at the second point regarding the use of confidential information. This is that members must not **appear** to use information that they have gained for their own personal advantage or that of a third party.

The point here is that even if the member is confident that he/she has not used confidential information for his/her own personal benefit or that of another, the member must also ensure that there is no possibility of anyone **thinking** that they have. It should not **appear** that the member has used confidential information inappropriately.

This is best illustrated with an example, using the same scenario as the last example.

> ### example
>
> **the danger of 'appearing' to pass on confidential information**
>
> We will now return to the example of Lubna Mirza that we looked at above. If Lubna follows the course of action recommended in the example she can be confident that she has not used confidential information about Richards Ltd to benefit her friend.
>
> Suppose that James Richards has completed the takeover of Lubna's friend's business and has paid £230,000 for it. If he were then to find out that the owner of the business he had bought was a close personal friend of Lubna's, he could quite legitimately question whether Lubna had passed on the information to her friend about what his maximum offer would be.
>
> What could Lubna do/have done to ensure that her duty of confidentiality was not called into question?
>
> As soon as she knew that James was intending to make an offer to buy her friend's business Lubna should have informed James of her relationship with the owner. She should also have explained to him that she is fully aware of her duty of confidentiality regarding information that she gains about a client and will not pass on any information. This would get her out of the dangerous situation where she could have 'appeared' to have advised the owner - simply because James would not have known otherwise.

the ongoing duty of confidentiality

We have already established that an accountant has an obligation to respect the confidentiality of information about employers or clients during the time that he/she is employed or is working for the client. This duty of confidentiality extends to the period **after the relationship has ended**.

Section 3.5.1 of the Guidelines states:

'the duty of confidentiality continues even after the end of the relationship between the member and the employer or client.'

In practice this means that any information that the accountant gains in the course of the professional work he/she carries out for a client remains confidential – even after the accountant is no longer employed by the client.

Similarly, information regarding an accountant's employer remains confidential even when the accountant moves to another employer.

DISCLOSURE OF CONFIDENTIAL INFORMATION

Having established that members have a duty of confidentiality, we will now look at the circumstances where confidential information can be disclosed. There are three main situations where it is acceptable to disclose confidential information. These are shown in the diagram below.

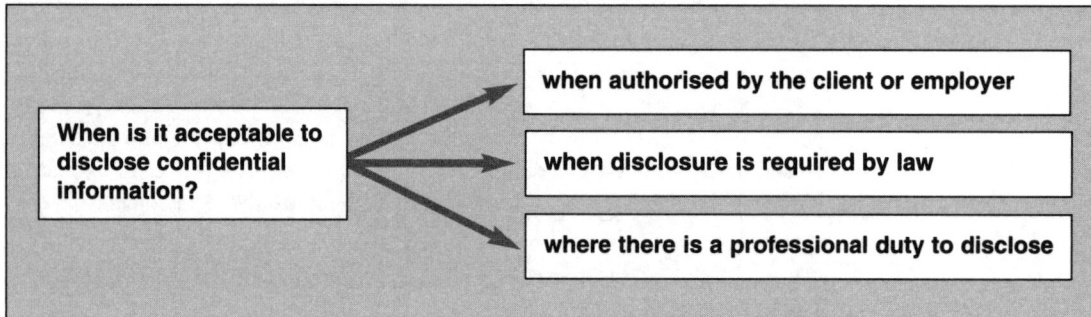

We will now look in more detail at these three situations.

authorised disclosure

In certain circumstances, the client or the employer may actually ask the accountant to disclose information that would otherwise have been treated as confidential.

The example that follows highlights a common situation where a client authorises the accountant to disclose confidential information to a third party.

---

example

authority to disclose

You work for a firm of accountants and receive a telephone call from a local builders' merchants asking for financial information about one of your clients who has requested to trade with them on credit.

How should you deal with this call?

Financial information regarding your client is confidential. Therefore you should not disclose any information about your client to the builders' merchants unless you have been authorised by the client to do so. You should contact your client to explain the situation and obtain specific authority to provide the financial information to the caller. Although verbal authority is acceptable, it would be better if this authority was given in writing.

When authority to disclose has been obtained from the client you can give the requested information to the builders' merchants. When doing this it is important include a disclaimer making it clear that this is for the use of the builders' merchants only and is given purely to help them to make a decision about whether or not to supply goods on credit to your client. You should also explain that the information is given without any financial responsibility on the part of yourself or the firm for which you work.

This example illustrates that where a client has given permission, the accountant is then able to disclose confidential information. The main point here is that the accountant must get specific authority from the client before doing so.

disclosure required by law

In some circumstances the accountant will be faced with a legal requirement to disclose confidential information. This legal requirement to disclose confidential information can be divided into two main categories:

■ where the information is required as evidence in a court of law

■ where the law requires that information must be revealed to the relevant authorities in situations where the law has been broken

This is illustrated in the diagram below.

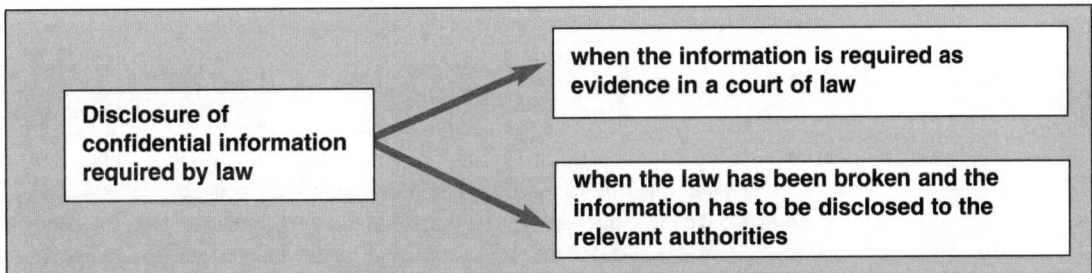

We will now look at each of these two requirements in more detail.

evidence in court

There may be circumstances where an accountant is required to provide evidence in a legal case in court. The accountant may receive a witness summons from the court and be required to:

■ provide documents which will be used in court as evidence, and/or

■ to appear in court in person to give evidence

Alternatively the member might be the subject of a court order requiring him or her to disclose confidential information about the client.

In any of these circumstances the member has a legal obligation to comply with the request. As a consequence the accountant must break his/her duty of confidentiality to the client or employer, even if the client or employer has refused to give permission for the evidence to be provided. The power of the law, through the witness summons or court order, is stronger and will prevail here.

The following example illustrates this point in practice.

example

a legal question of confidentiality

Rachael Thomas acts as the accountant for Rolls Ltd. One of Rolls Ltd's suppliers has taken them to court for failure to pay for goods that have been supplied to them. There has been an ongoing dispute between Rolls and this supplier which has resulted in the non-payment by Rolls.

Rachael has been asked to provide copies of all documents relevant to this dispute, including invoices and correspondence, as evidence in the case. She has also been told that she may be required to appear in court as a witness to give evidence.

In these circumstances what steps should Rachael take before providing this information?

The information that Rachael has been asked to provide to the court is confidential. The first thing that she should do is to make her client, Rolls Ltd, aware that she expects to be called as a witness thereby giving them the opportunity to give her authority to provide the information in court. If they agree then she is free to provide the relevant documents or evidence as requested.

If, despite being informed of Rachael's likely appearance in court, Rolls Ltd refuses to give authority for her to disclose then Rachael must wait until she receives a witness summons. When this occurs she is legally required to comply with the summons and provide the relevant documentation, and if necessary, appear in court herself to give evidence.

disclosure where infringement of the law has occurred

Where a client or an employer has broken the law there may be a requirement for the accountant to disclose information to the relevant authorities that would otherwise be considered confidential.

A good example of this is in relation to money laundering.

A definition of money laundering is:

'to move illegally acquired cash through financial systems so that it appears to be legally acquired.'

Basically, as the name 'money laundering' suggests, when the money has been gained through illegal activities it is seen as 'dirty money'. By using that money in legitimate trade or investment activities this is like 'washing' or 'laundering' the money so that it then appears to be 'clean' and legally obtained.

The current legislation relating to money laundering is the **Criminal Justice Act 1993**. It requires accountants to report immediately any suspicion that they have that money has been gained from illegal activities to the National Criminal Intelligence Service (NCIS).

Money laundering is covered in detail in Chapter 7. It is clear that in the circumstances described here the accountant has to disclose confidential information about a client if he/she considers that the client has broken the law.

a professional duty to disclose

In certain circumstances, an accountant may have a **professional duty** to disclose confidential information. Section 3.5.6 (iii) of the Guidelines identifies three areas where there is a professional duty:

'(a) *to comply with technical standards and ethical requirements*

(b) *to protect the professional interests of the member in legal proceedings*

(c) *to respond to an inquiry by the AAT or by a regulatory body of an ethical, investigatory or disciplinary nature'*

We will look briefly at each of these three points. At this stage in your studies it is sufficient that you are aware that there are certain circumstances in which a member of the AAT has a professional duty to disclose confidential information. You would not be expected to know this area of the Guidelines in great detail.

In point (a) an accountant has a professional duty to disclose confidential information in order **to comply with technical standards and ethical requirements**. Technical standards in this case refer to International Accounting Standards (IASs), Standard Statements of Accounting Practice (SSAPs), Financial Reporting Standards (FRSs) and other relevant standards. Ethical requirements are those set out in the AAT Guidelines on Professional Ethics referred to regularly in this text.

Secondly, in point (b), an accountant has a professional duty to disclose if he/she is to protect his/her professional interests in legal proceedings. If, for example, an accountant was faced with legal action against him/her by a client, he/she would be permitted to disclose otherwise confidential information to protect his/her professional good name.

Lastly, in point (c), a professional accountant must disclose confidential information if it is in response **to an inquiry by the AAT or by a regulatory body of an ethical, investigatory or disciplinary nature**. This inquiry could be in relation to the actions of the member in question, or an inquiry relating to an investigation into the actions of another member. If the member finds that in order to respond to the inquiry from the AAT he/she must disclose information that would otherwise have been seen as confidential, he/she has a professional duty to disclose this.

This type of situation could arise where the AAT has received a complaint from a client of one of its members regarding the fee that they have been charged for accounts work that the member has carried out. The AAT has a duty to investigate this complaint. In order to answer the questions that the AAT raises with him/her the member may have to disclose confidential client information to the AAT relating to the work that he/she has carried out.

the decision to disclose

If a member makes the decision to disclose confidential information, there are three points in section 3.5.7 of the Guidelines which must be considered before making this disclosure. These points can be summarised as follows:

■ The member must decide whether he/she knows all the facts regarding the issue and has enough evidence to back up these facts. If he/she does not have enough evidence then the member must use his/her professional judgement to decide to what extent (if any) the confidential information can be disclosed.

■ Next, the member must decide who is the right person(s) to whom this information should be disclosed, and also how it should be communicated, for example by letter, report or verbally. This decision should ensure that the person provided with the information has the necessary authority to act upon it.

■ Finally, the member must consider whether he/she would face any legal consequences from disclosing confidential information, and if so how serious these consequences could be.

We can see that the AAT takes the subject of disclosure of confidential information very seriously and members must be very careful when deciding whether or not they should disclose.

In any circumstances where a member is unsure whether or not they should disclose confidential information, or where they are unclear as to how much they should disclose, they should consider taking legal advice from a solicitor or contact the AAT Ethics Advice Line. It is always better to get a second opinion if there is any doubt over the action that should be taken, rather than risk making the wrong decision.

TAXATION SERVICES

One of the main professional services that members of the accountancy profession provide to their clients is taxation (tax) services. As you may know from your studies or experience, dealing with the tax affairs of an individual or a business can be very complex. Consequently many organisations rely on the professional expertise of accountants to deal with their tax.

The AAT covers ethical issues relating to the provision of taxation services by its members in section 3.6 of the Guidelines. It is recognised in the Guidelines that taxation is a complex area and it states in section 3.6.2 that

'it is beyond the scope of these guidelines to deal with detailed ethical issues relating to taxation services encountered by members.'

Where detailed advice in this area is required, the Guidelines suggest that the member should telephone the AAT Ethics Advice Line.

ethics and taxation services

There are two main types of taxation:

- indirect taxation such as Value Added Tax (VAT)
- direct taxation including taxes on income, profits and other gains (eg capital gains)

The guidance that the Guidelines give in Section 3.6 is general and applies to both direct and indirect taxes. If you want to refer to the full text of the Guidelines, it is set out in Appendix I (see page 179).

These points from the Guidelines have been summarised in the table which follows (pages 43-46). The table refers to the section of the Guidelines where the information can be found, provides a summary of the point concerned and an explanation of how it might work in practice. You should read through these points for reference. Please note that you will not have to remember all these details in your assessment, but should concentrate on the main principles illustrated in the example on page 46.

summary of the AAT Guidelines relating to tax services	explanation of the ethical point in practice
3.6.4 When providing tax services to a client or employer, **members have a duty to put forward the best position for the client** provided it is consistent with the law and does not threaten the integrity or objectivity of the member.	Many clients expect their accountant to be able to reduce their tax bill. Members must explain to their clients that they will always try to ensure they do not pay any more tax than they are required to. However they cannot guarantee a reduction in tax, as each client is different.

summary of the AAT Guidelines relating to tax services	explanation of the ethical point in practice
3.6.5 A member must make it clear to their client or employer that the tax return that he/she has prepared or the advice that has been given is **an expression of opinion and not statement of fact.**	Clients or employers will often believe that if a professionally qualified accountant prepares their tax return then it must be right. They consequently do not expect for there to be any problems once it is submitted to the relevant tax authorities. However, this is not the case and it is important for the accountant to explain that the tax authorities could challenge the information that has been submitted.
3.6.6 When taking on tax work for a client or employer the member must act in good faith and exercise care. However, it is normally assumed that information on which the tax return is based has been provided by the client and ultimately **the accuracy of information included in a tax return lies with the tax payer** rather than the member.	It must be made clear to the client that the accountant will use all his/her technical skills and expertise to perform tax calculations and complete tax returns for the client. However, the client bears the final responsibility for the information provided. Therefore it is no defence for a client to blame his/her accountant if the relevant tax authorities identify that information provided to them was incorrect.
3.6.7 Where a member submits a tax return for the client or employer he/she is then **acting as an agent** for them. It is very important that the member makes his/her responsibilities as their agent very clear to the client or employer.	Part of the role of an accountant will involve dealing with the tax authorities on behalf of the client or employer and submitting their tax returns. In this situation the accountant is acting as an agent, and so the primary liability (responsibility) for the tax return lies with the client or employer. The duties of the accountant should be clarified in the engagement letter signed by the client and the accountant at the start of the assignment. (Engagement letters are covered in detail on pages 88-90).
3.6.8 Any **tax advice** that a member gives to a client or employer **should be properly recorded** in the form of a letter to a client or a memo to an employer.	In addition to carrying out tax calculations and preparing tax returns, accountants will often provide their clients or employers with tax advice. The accountant should ensure that this advice is suitably documented – so that if there were to be any disagreement in the future regarding the nature of the advice the accountant would have documentary proof if required.

summary of the AAT Guidelines relating to tax services	explanation of the ethical point in practice
3.6.9 **A member should not be associated with any tax return or communication** with the tax authorities if they believe that it: ■ contains false or misleading information ■ contains information that has been included without full consideration as to whether it is true or false ■ leaves out or hides information that should be submitted to the extent that it could mislead the tax authorities	An accountant who is involved in preparing a tax return will do his/her best to ensure that the information included in the return is accurate and where an error is found he/she will correct it. However, if the client or employer insists on submitting information that the accountant knows to be false he/she should refuse to deal with it. Similarly if the accountant believes that information in the return cannot be properly justified or if certain relevant information has been left out, he/she should refuse to deal with it.
3.6.10 Where a member in practice is acting for a client, **the client should be given copies of all tax computations** before they are submitted to the relevant tax authorities.	Although clients are keen to pass on the responsibility for preparing tax computations and submitting tax returns to their accountants it is important that the accountant always provides the client with a copy of the computations before they are sent to the tax authorities. This will allow the client to have a look at and check the figures, if they wish, and to then ask the accountant any questions they have about the figures or how the calculations have been performed.
3.6.11 If an accountant spots that there is a material error or omission in a previous year's tax return or that a return has not been submitted, this should be pointed out immediately to the client or employer with **a recommendation to disclose the error or omission**. If the client or employer decides not to correct the error then the accountant should no longer act for them.	Accountants regularly review previous years' tax returns for a number of reasons such as taking on a new client or when information has come to light that could affect the previous year's return. If they identify errors or omissions in the previous returns they cannot simply ignore them and should report them to the client or employer, explaining the error, identifying the consequences and recommending that the error is disclosed to the relevant authorities immediately. But the accountant should not disclose this matter to the authorities unless they have been given permission by the client or employer. If the client or employer does not correct the error then the accountant should tell them that he/she can no longer act for them.

summary of the AAT Guidelines relating to tax services	explanation of the ethical point in practice
3.6.12 **If a self-employed member identifies an error which a client then refuses to disclose to the tax authorities the member should cease to act for the client** and inform the tax authorities that they are no longer acting for the client. In certain circumstances the member should also inform the authorities that the member has information that indicates that the accounts and statements etc. of the client should not be relied upon.	This point highlights the fact that a self-employed member may be faced with the same issue as in 3.6.11 above, where a client decides not to disclose an error or omission in a previous year's tax return. They have in this case additional responsibilities.
	In this situation they must tell the client in writing that they will no longer act for them. They must also tell the Revenue that they have stopped acting for the client. If they were the accountants who actually prepared the tax information in question they should also inform the tax authorities that the information in the accounts can no longer be relied upon.

the importance of the Guidelines

We can see from the above table that where accountants perform tax computations, complete tax returns and/or provide tax advice there are a number of ethical points to consider. Provided that they adhere to the guidance in section 3.6 of the Guidelines they will, in most cases, maintain the expected professional standards and will not compromise honesty and integrity when dealing with a client or an employee's tax matters.

example

a question of tax

A potential new tax client, John Sinclair, makes the following statement: 'The reason I chose your firm is because you saved my friend loads of tax and he didn't even have to check all the paperwork you gave him!'

What points should you raise with John in reply to this statement?

Your explanation should cover the following points:

■ Although you will try to ensure that John pays no more tax than required, you cannot guarantee a reduction in the amount he pays, because all clients are different.

■ Final responsibility for the accuracy of information in the tax return lies with John.

■ John will be provided with a copy of the tax return and relevant calculations to check and can then ask any questions before it is submitted to the tax authorities.

■ It is always possible that the tax authorities could challenge the information that is submitted.

Chapter
Summary

- Accountants have an obligation to respect the confidentiality of information about a client's or employer's affairs acquired in the course of professional work.

- Accountants must ensure that any staff who work for them also follow the principle of confidentiality.

- Confidential information should not be used or appear to be used for the personal advantage of the member or a third party.

- The duty of confidentiality continues after the end of the relationship between the accountant and the employer or client.

- Confidential information can be disclosed when a client or employer authorises the disclosure.

- If the law specifically requires it confidential information about a client or employer can be disclosed.

- If an accountant has a professional duty to either comply with accounting standards, protect his/her professional interests in legal proceedings or respond to an AAT inquiry, confidential information may be disclosed.

- When accountants are carrying out tax services for clients or employers they must ensure that they put the best case for the client without breaking the law or compromising their integrity or objectivity.

- Ultimate responsibility for the tax affairs of a client or employer remains with the client or employer and not with the accountant.

- An accountant should not be associated with a tax return if he/she believes that it contains false information or omits relevant information.

- If an accountant discovers a material error or omission in a previous tax return he/she should recommend that the client discloses this error to the relevant tax authorities immediately.

- If the client or employer decides not to disclose an error or omission the accountant should cease to act for them.

- If an accountant requires advice on detailed ethical issues he/she should contact the AAT Ethics Advice Line.

<table>
<tr><td rowspan="10">**Key Terms**</td></tr>
</table>

duty of confidentiality	the accountant's obligation to respect confidential information about the client or employer's affairs
ongoing duty of confidentiality	the fact that the accountant's duty of confidentiality continues even after the end of the relationship between the accountant and the employer or client
authorised disclosure	disclosure of confidential information by an accountant following authorisation by the client or employer
disclosure required by law	the legal requirement for an accountant to disclose financial information about a client or an employer
money laundering	to move illegally acquired cash through financial systems so that it appears to be legally acquired
NCIS	National Criminal Investigation Service
indirect taxation	a tax on goods and services such as Value Added Tax (VAT)
direct taxation	a tax on an individual or company such as income tax and corporation tax
tax return	an official form from HM Revenue & Customs on which an individual or company enters details of income and expenditure which are then used to assess a tax liability

Student Activities

answers to the asterisked (*) questions are to be found at the back of this book.

3.1* You work for a firm of accountants as an audit supervisor. Two juniors who work in your office, Pierre and Jane, are having the following conversation in the entrance hall of the office building that your firm shares with four other companies.

Pierre – 'I've just finished working on Booth Ltd's accounts. I bet Mrs Booth is really cross that the company's profit is down 25% on last year. She's so unpleasant, it serves her right!'

Jane – 'I know what you mean I hate working for unpleasant clients. Where I used to work I had a client called Castle & Co. Peter Castle was a horrid man, he used to only pay his staff the minimum wage but paid himself £120,000 last year.

What ethical issues are raised by the conversation between Pierre and Jane? Does it make any difference that Pierre was discussing a current client and Jane a client for whom she no longer works?

3.2* (a) What are the main circumstances in which it is acceptable for an accountant to disclose confidential information about a client or employer?

(b) If an accountant is in any doubt about whether to disclose confidential information, what should he/she do?

3.3* You work in the purchase ledger section of Lambretti & Clarke. You have just approached a new supplier for the supply of goods on thirty days credit and have asked for a credit limit of £70,000. As part of their credit checking procedures the supplier has requested a copy of your accounts for the last two years and bank details of the company to allow them to request a bank reference.

What action should you take before providing them with this information?

3.4 You work as an assistant accountant for Jones & Udal and have been notified that you may be called as a witness in a court case involving one of your clients. Your firm has also been required to provide certain confidential documents as evidence for the case.

What steps should you and Jones & Udal take before giving evidence and providing the necessary documentation as evidence?

3.5 One of the main areas of business that the firm that you work for is involved in is the preparation of tax returns. The partners have asked you to produce a checklist for all members of staff to use to ensure that when preparing tax returns for clients they comply with the ethical standards set out in the AAT Guidelines.

Ethics and the employed accountant

This chapter focuses specifically on the ethical guidance that the AAT gives to its members who are employees – in industry, commerce, the public sector or in public practice.

This chapter covers:

■ conflict of loyalty to the employer and to the accounting profession

■ whistleblowing

■ the need for an accountant to support professional colleagues

■ professional competence needed by an employed member

PERFORMANCE CRITERIA COVERED

unit 32: PROFESSIONAL ETHICS

Element 32.2:

develop, maintain and apply ethics in employer/employee situations

A   Describe the type of culture within organisations which supports and promotes high ethical values and helps resolve any conflict of loyalties.

B   Resolve conflicting loyalties where an employer may ask you to perform tasks which are illegal, unethical or against the rules or standards of the accounting profession.

C   Follow appropriate procedures where you believe an employer has or will commit an act you believe to be illegal or unethical.

D   Respond appropriately to requests to work outside the confines of your own professional experience and expertise.

INTRODUCTION

Much of the emphasis of the AAT Guidelines on Professional Ethics relates to guidance for members in practice – ie members who provide accounting and other services to clients on a self-employed basis. However, if you think about the qualified members of the AAT that you know, you will realise that probably the majority of them are employed in industry, commerce, the public sector, or in public practice.

Section 4 of the Guidelines provides specific ethical guidance for employed members. Sections 1-3 are also relevant as they are applicable to all members (see diagram on page 5).

Section 4 covers three main areas which are:

- conflict of loyalties
- support for professional colleagues
- professional competence

We will now examine each of these in turn.

CONFLICT OF LOYALTIES

a definition of loyalty

One definition of loyalty is:

'being firm and not changing in your support for a person or an organisation, or in your belief in your principles.'

Society generally views loyalty as a good thing whether it is to friends, family or to employers. Employers are keen for their employees to be loyal to the organisation that they work for as this encourages stability within the workforce and a good team spirit, which in turn contributes to the success of the organisation. It also means that employees will be supportive of decisions taken by the organisation that they work for and will carry out the tasks that are expected of them.

One of the factors that will help to maintain an employee's loyalty to the organisation that he/she works for is a culture that encourages strong ethical values. We have seen in previous chapters just how important the AAT considers ethics to be for its members. But this need for strong ethical values is not limited to the accountancy profession. Every employee, regardless of their seniority in an organisation, should maintain an ethical approach to their work.

conflict of loyalties

Employed members of the AAT are expected to be loyal to their employer; but, as members of the AAT, they also owe a duty of loyalty to their profession. There is potential for conflict here.

Section 4.2.1 of the Guidelines states that:

'Employed members owe a duty of loyalty to their employer as well as to their profession and there may be times when the two are in conflict. An employee's normal priority should be to support his or her organisation's legitimate and ethical objectives and the rules and procedures drawn up in support of them.'

What does this mean in practical terms? In the first instance the member must remain loyal to his/her employer provided that the organisation is acting in a legal and ethical way. However, there may be times when something that the employer expects the member to do conflicts with the member's professional and ethical values.

The Guidelines specifically state in Section 4.2.1 that

'an employee cannot legitimately be required to:

(i)   break the law;

(ii)   breach the rules and standards of their profession;

(iii) lie or mislead (including by keeping silent) those acting as auditors to the employer; or

(iv) put their name to or otherwise be associated with a statement which materially misrepresents the facts.'

We can see that all of the above are very serious situations. Each one clearly conflicts with the ethical standards expected of a professional accountant.

Breaking the law is obviously not something anyone, never mind a professional accountant, should do. The rules and standards of the accounting professional are clearly there for a purpose and should not be broken by members of the profession. Note that breaching ethical standards includes not only active deception, as in point (iv), but also a member misleading auditors by just keeping quiet when he/she knows the auditors have got something wrong, as in point (iii).

So what happens if a member is put in a position where the employer expects him/her to do one (or more) of the above? Sections 4.2.2 - 4.2.5 of the AAT Guidelines explain what an employed member should do when faced with these situations. This can be summarised as follows:

- If the employer has broken the law, the member should try hard to persuade the employer not to continue with the unlawful activity and to rectify the situation as soon as possible.

- If there is a difference of opinion between the member and the employer regarding an accounting or ethical matter, wherever possible this should be resolved with the involvement of more senior staff within the organisation. If necessary, the issue should be brought to the attention of senior management and ultimately if all else fails, at non-executive director level.

- Where the issue between the employer and the member cannot be resolved and the member considers that he/she has exhausted all other possible alternatives then he/she may have no option but to offer to resign. In this case the employed member should explain to the employer the reasons for his/her resignation, and should at the same time maintain the duty of confidentiality to the employer.

It is worth noting here that the AAT strongly recommends that the member should obtain legal advice before taking the step of offering to resign. One important reason for this is that the law now protects an employee from dismissal for 'whistleblowing', ie breaking confidentiality (see next section). In other words, the employee should not have to be put in the position of having to lose his/her job when the matter is serious enough to be made public. Only the AAT or a lawyer (or both) can advise in this situation.

The process of dealing with conflicts of loyalty is summarised in the diagram below.

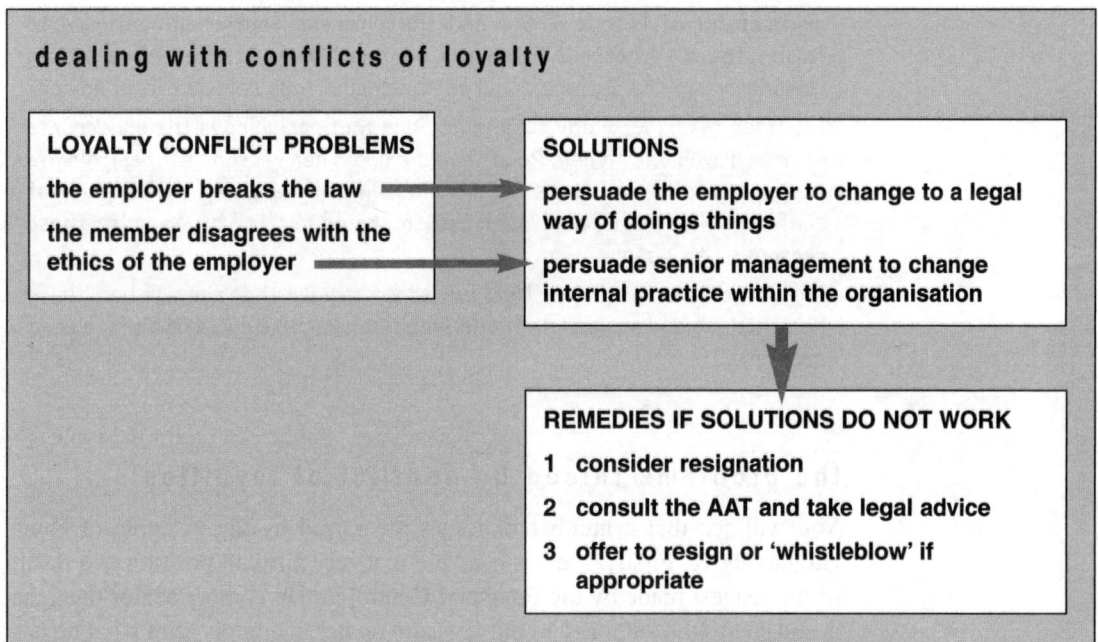

dealing with conflicts of loyalty

LOYALTY CONFLICT PROBLEMS

the employer breaks the law

the member disagrees with the ethics of the employer

SOLUTIONS

persuade the employer to change to a legal way of doings things

persuade senior management to change internal practice within the organisation

REMEDIES IF SOLUTIONS DO NOT WORK

1 consider resignation

2 consult the AAT and take legal advice

3 offer to resign or 'whistleblow' if appropriate

The area of conflict of loyalties and the ethical issues that it raises is illustrated in the example that follows.

example

a conflict of loyalties

Rona Hughes works as an accounts assistant in the accounts department of Peters & Son where one of her responsibilities is to prepare the quarterly VAT return for the company. It is now the end of the financial year and the Financial Controller has asked Rona to manipulate the figures to be included on the VAT return so that the company's year-end VAT liability is reduced.

This is clearly wrong and Rona should take no part in the Financial Controller's request to falsify the data that is to be included in the VAT return. But what should she do in these circumstances to resolve the problem?

As an employee of Peters & Son, Rona has a duty of loyalty to the company and to the Financial Controller as her line manager, but she also has a duty of loyalty to the accountancy profession.

In this case there is a conflict of loyalty between the two. In the first instance, Rona should explain to the Financial Controller that she has serious concerns about doing what he has asked and cannot be involved in such activities. If, at this point, the Financial Controller agrees with Rona that she is right, then no further action needs to be taken. However if, despite raising her concerns with him, there is still a disagreement, Rona would have to raise the issue with a higher level of management.

Finally, if Rona has no success when she raises the matter with the senior management of Peters & Son and the Financial Controller continues to falsify the VAT records, Rona will be faced with no alternative but to consider resigning. Before doing so she should take relevant legal advice.

If, after taking legal advice, she decides that resigning is the only course of action available to her, Rona should explain her reasons for resigning to the management at Peters & Son. She will still be bound by her duty of confidentiality to her employer and so should not tell anyone else these reasons at this stage.

If, on the other hand, her legal advisors consider that she will be able to keep her job and suggest that she 'whistleblows', she could do so (see next section).

the problems raised by conflict of loyalties

You will see that a number of issues are raised by the example of Rona Hughes above. Firstly, she has been put in a very difficult position as a result of the request made by the Financial Controller. He is more senior than she is and so has the authority to put pressure on her to comply with what he has asked her to do. Raising the issue with more senior management in the organisation is likely to cause a significant amount of tension between the Financial Controller and Rona, which could ultimately make her position within Peters & Son very difficult.

Resigning from the company would also be a huge step for Rona to take. The consequences of this could be that she may not receive a reference from Peters & Son, or may find it difficult to find another job.

With all these issues to contend with it is easy to see why some employees choose to remain silent about malpractices that occur within their organisation. They choose instead, to 'keep their heads down' and ignore the ethical issues that this raises.

whistleblowing

We saw from the section above and the example of Rona Hughes that the final option open to an employed member of the AAT when faced with a serious conflict of loyalties is to resign. In these circumstances the member continues to be bound by the duty of confidentiality that they have to their employer. However, some employed members may choose not to remain silent and may decide to 'blow the whistle' on the organisation that employs them where they have good reason to believe that illegal or unethical practices are occurring. In the case of Rona she may decide that she is not prepared to resign and 'go quietly'. Instead, after taking legal advice, she may decide to report Peters & Son to the relevant authorities.

So what do we mean by the term 'whistleblowing'? A whistleblower can be defined as:

'a person who tells someone in authority about something illegal that is happening within the organisation for which they work.'

This can be a very serious step especially if the employee decides not to resign after blowing the whistle. In these circumstances the employer is unlikely to be very happy if one of its employees has reported them for something illegal and are unlikely to want the person to work for them any longer. Consequently is it important that the employee has some protection from dismissal if they choose to blow the whistle on the employer.

The Public Interest Disclosure Act, 1998 (PIDA) offers the employee such protection in certain circumstances. The PIDA (which is sometimes referred to as 'the Whistleblowers Charter') gives an employee protection where he/she discloses otherwise confidential information which he/she reasonably believes shows that one of the following has or is likely to occur:

■ a criminal offence

■ a breach of a legal obligation

- a miscarriage of justice
- a breach of public safety legislation
- environmental damage

In order to be protected from dismissal the employee must also be able to show that:

- the disclosure is made in good faith
- the employee reasonably believes that the information disclosed is true
- the employee would otherwise be victimised or the evidence concealed or destroyed if the information is not disclosed

The Public Interest Disclosure Act, 1998 does make it easier for an employee to report an unethical or disreputable employer, but it still cannot offer complete protection from the employer who is the target of the whistleblowing. Recent cases of whistleblowing have resulted in employees being suspended pending an enquiry, or being dismissed at a later date for some unconnected reason. The main risk for an individual who has blown the whistle on an employer is the subsequent effect on future career prospects.

The following example highlights the serious consequences of deciding to 'blow the whistle' on an employer.

example

time to blow the whistle?

Stephanie Andrews works as an accountant for Harmsworthy Plc, a large quoted company. The Finance Director has asked her to help her with a scheme which she and the Managing Director have come up with. The directors have offered to pay Stephanie £5,000 for her help in the scheme which involves illegal dealing in shares of Harmsworthy. The Finance Director has made it clear to Stephanie that if she does not help them she will lose her job.

What should Stephanie do in this situation?

An employee cannot legitimately be required to break the law by his/her employer. In the first instance, Stephanie should raise her concerns with the directors of Harmsworthy and make every effort to persuade them not to break the law. However, this option could prove difficult for Stephanie as it is the senior management of Harmsworthy who are involved in the illegal activity.

Assuming Stephanie does not agree to break the law she is faced with two options. First, she could choose to resign from Harmsworthy stating her reasons for doing so. Secondly, she may decide to blow the whistle on the management of Harmsworthy and report them to the appropriate authorities. Under the second option she must be sure that the facts are correct and that she would be victimised and the evidence concealed or destroyed if she did not whistleblow.

This example highlights just how difficult it can be to make the decision to 'blow the whistle' and disclose confidential information about an employer.

For further reading, visit the AAT website (www.aat.org.uk) and read the article '*The Ethics of Whistleblowing*' (use the word 'whistleblowing' in the site search facility to access it). This article summarises the main points that must be considered when deciding whether to contact the relevant authorities and whistleblow on an employer. The main points are summarised in the questions and answers in the table below.

SO WHAT DO I NEED TO THINK ABOUT BEFORE I WHISTLEBLOW?	
Q	**A**
Are you sure that you are fully aware of the facts and do you have some evidence to support the facts?	There is nothing worse than going down the whistleblowing route only to be told later that there was a reasonable explanation for something that you were concerned about.
Do you have internal procedures within the organisation that you have to follow to make a disclosure of malpractice?	If this is the case, you should consider using these procedures. Also, refer to the AAT Guidelines on Professional Ethics.
Have you explained the situation fully to management, ie your concerns and how the organisation could be affected by not addressing them?	Your explanations could help the organisation to understand the short-term and long-term implications of the problems you have highlighted.
Do you wish to obtain general and professional advice about what you are proposing to do?	It would be a good idea to contact bodies such as a trade union or the AAT.
Do you want to take legal advice?	Try a local Law Centre or Citizens Advice Bureau.
and last but not least . . . Have you thought fully about the consequences of blowing the whistle?	Your future career prospects may be in danger if you do not think the matter through and take appropriate advice.

This table shows that the decision to blow the whistle on an employer is a very serious step. Statistics show that whistleblowing is on the increase. Employees are increasingly less likely to allow unethical and illegal practices to continue in the organisations for which they work. Accountants must ensure that they always promote best practice and by doing so encourage their colleagues to maintain high ethical standards.

SUPPORT OF PROFESSIONAL COLLEAGUES

supporting working relationships

In any job, employees are likely to have to work with other employees. Employed members of the AAT will most likely work within the accounting department of the organisation for which they work. Within this department there may be other qualified accountants, trainee accountants and members of staff who, although not qualified, will have a great deal of accounting experience.

The relationships between the members of an accounts team may depend on qualified accountants having seniority and therefore authority over other members, in other words the junior members of staff work for and report to a more senior qualified person.

One important aspect of these relationships is that the junior members of staff should have the opportunity to develop and make their own decisions on accounting matters. They should also be encouraged to form their own opinions on accounting matters even if ultimately these are found to be incorrect.

Section 4.3 of the Guidelines makes the following statement in relation to this aspect of support of professional colleagues.

'A member, particularly one having authority over others, should give due weight to the need for them to develop and hold their own judgement in accounting matters and should deal with differences of opinion in a professional way.'

The key points here are that when dealing with more junior members of staff, members of the AAT should:

- allow other, more junior, members of staff to develop and use their own judgement in accounting matters
- deal with differences of opinion between themselves and other, more junior, colleagues in a professional way

The next two examples clearly highlight each of these points in practice.

example

a question of delegation

Stephen Boyd is the Senior Accountant for Brains Ltd, and is responsible for a team of 12 within the finance department of the company. He is more qualified than all of his staff both professionally and by experience, but despite the pressures of his job, he finds it difficult to delegate any of the more complex work to members of his team.

Rebecca Luebke is one of the assistant accountants in Stephen's team and has recently qualified as a member of the AAT. She is keen to put the skills that she has developed during her studies into practice and has asked Stephen if she could prepare the depreciation schedules for the year-end accounts. Fixed assets and depreciation is an area that Stephen always works on himself.

What should Stephen do in this situation?

Stephen is obviously uncomfortable delegating any of his responsibility to members of his team. But as an accountant he has a professional responsibility to allow colleagues to develop and use their own judgement in accounting matters. Therefore, Stephen should welcome Rebecca's enthusiasm to take on a new challenge and should allow her to carry out the work on depreciation. He should, however, ensure that he gives her adequate guidance on how the work should be performed.

When Rebecca has completed her work Stephen should ensure that he checks it and that he gives Rebecca constructive feedback on the work she has performed.

This example highlights the first key point of the AAT guidance on support for professional colleagues (see bullet points on previous page). This states that AAT members should allow their colleagues to **develop and use their own judgement in accounting matters**. In the example above Rebecca will get a tremendous sense of achievement if she is allowed to carry out the work on depreciation and will have developed her own accounting skills at the same time.

The next example looks at the second key point of the AAT guidance on support for professional colleagues: dealing with differences in opinion in a professional manner.

example

a difference of opinion

Hugo Ross is the Financial Controller and Geraint Williams is a senior accountant in the accounts department of Henry Charles Ltd. Hugo is generally a very loud character and tends to shout at his staff and always gets his own way. At the end of the year Geraint has given Hugo a detailed schedule calculating the provision for bad debts which he has prepared.

Hugo marches into the office and shouts at Geraint that the calculation has been performed on a totally incorrect basis and that instead of being based on 5% of all debts over six months old it should be 3% of the whole debtor balance. When Geraint tries to reply Hugo tells him to 'shut up' and to change the figures on the revised basis he has indicated.

Has Hugo dealt with this situation correctly?

Hugo has completely dismissed Geraint's work without giving Geraint any opportunity to explain his calculations. This is not a professional way to deal with a colleague. Hugo should have taken Geraint into his office and asked him to explain the basis of his calculations. If Hugo still does not agree with Geraint, he should explain why he feels his basis for the calculation is more appropriate. If Hugo still considers that his method is more appropriate after discussing the issue in full he should then use his authority and state that his method of calculation should be used.

The important point to draw from this example is that accountants must ensure that they deal with differences of opinion in a professional manner and do not use a position of seniority to override the opinion of more junior staff.

PROFESSIONAL COMPETENCE

One of the fundamental ethical principles introduced in Chapter 1 was **professional and technical competence**. Section 2.3.1 of the Guidelines states:

'Members should refrain from undertaking or continuing any assignments which they are not competent to carry out unless advice and assistance is obtained to ensure that the assignment is carried out satisfactorily.'

This point is covered again in Section 4.4 of the Guidelines specifically in relation to employed members:

'A member employed in industry, commerce, the public sector or education may be asked to undertake significant tasks for which he or she has not had sufficient specific training or experience. When undertaking such work the member should not mislead the employer as to the degree of expertise or experience he or she possesses, and where appropriate expert advice, assistance or training should be sought.'

In each of these sections of the Guidelines it is clear that members are expected to take advice, assistance or training if they do not have the necessary skills to carry out an assignment or task that they have been asked to complete. The main difference here is the point that *'the member should not mislead the employer as to the degree of expertise or experience he or she possesses'*.

We will now explore what this point means in more detail.

Many employees are ambitious and keen to progress within the organisation for which they work. Therefore, when there is an opportunity to do some more challenging work, this can be seen by employees as a way to show their ability and make a name for themselves. In this situation there can sometimes be a temptation for an employee to 'talk up' his/her experience and ability to perform the work in question in order to persuade the employer that he/she is the 'right person for the job'.

In the case of members of the AAT it is important that they should not exaggerate their own expertise or experience in relation to accounting skills. If an employed AAT member tells his/her employer that they have the necessary skills and expertise to carry out a particular task when they do not, this can have much more serious consequences.

This point is illustrated in the following example.

example

a question of experience

When Amit Odedra joined the accounts department of Warwick & Parks six months ago, he made it clear at his interview that he was very ambitious and keen to progress within the company. Mike Smith, the Finance Director, has noticed that Amit is very hard working and is regularly the last person to leave the office. He has therefore asked Amit to take on responsibility for preparing the monthly payroll for the company.

Amit has never done any payroll work before but would really like to take on the additional responsibility. What should Amit do in this situation?

Amit is very keen to progress within Warwick & Parks, but as a member of the AAT he should be aware that ethically he must not mislead his employer about the extent of his expertise and experience. Consequently, he should explain to Mike that whilst he is keen to take on the extra responsibility, he has no previous experience in payroll and so would need some training in this area before he could perform the additional work.

If Amit did not make Mike aware of this and took on the additional responsibility of payroll without any training, the implications for Warwick & Parks could be very serious. Firstly, it is likely that the payroll would be incorrectly prepared which could mean (if the error was not picked up) that staff were paid the wrong amounts. Secondly, calculations of Pay As You Earn (PAYE) and National Insurance (NI) for payment to the Her Majesty's Revenue & Customs (HMRC) could be incorrect which could ultimately result in the company being fined.

We can see from this example that the fundamental principle of professional and technical competence is very relevant to the employed member. It would be ethically wrong for an employed member of the AAT to mislead the employer as to his/her expertise and experience. Errors could result which would have serious consequences for the employer.

■ Employed AAT members have a duty of loyalty to the organisation that employs them.

■ Employed members also have a duty of loyalty to the accounting profession.

■ Sometimes the loyalty to employer and the loyalty to profession may conflict.

■ Where an employed member believes that the employer is doing something illegal or unethical he/she should make every effort to persuade the employer to stop.

■ If the employer does not stop the issue should be raised with more senior management or, ultimately, the non-executive directors of the organisation.

■ If this does not resolve the issue, the member may have no alternative but to consider resigning.

■ Before resigning the AAT strongly recommend that an employed member should obtain legal advice.

■ Members may decide to whistleblow on their employers where they feel that serious malpractice is occurring.

■ Providing a member is acting in good faith when they 'blow the whistle' on an employer and so break the duty of confidentiality, he/she will be protected in many situations by the Public Interest Disclosure Act.

■ It is therefore recommended that members should consider taking legal advice before deciding to whistleblow on their organisation.

■ Members should always give support to their professional colleagues by allowing them to develop their own judgement on accounting matters and by dealing with differences of opinion in a professional way.

■ Employed members should not mislead their employers as to the degree of expertise or experience that they have.

■ Members should always seek expert advice, assistance or training where they do not have the necessary skills or experience to complete a task which they have been asked to carry out.

Key Terms		
	loyalty	being firm and not changing in support for a person or an organisation
	conflict of loyalties	this arises where an employee's loyalty to his/her employer clashes with his/her loyalty to the accounting profession
	whistleblowing	telling someone in authority about something illegal that is happening within the organisation that an employee works for
	Public Interest Disclosure Act 1998	an Act of Parliament to protect employees who make disclosures of confidential information that they believe to be in the public interest
	professional competence	the duty of members to ensure that they have the necessary skills to carry out any work that they are required to carry out; members should not mislead their employers as to the degree of expertise or experience that they have

Student Activities

answers to the
asterisked (*)
questions are to
be found at the
back of this book.

4.1* You are employed as an assistant accountant at Flowmow Ltd, a company that manufactures lawnmowers. Your accounts supervisor passes a batch of invoices to you to process. You are unable to match two of the invoices to either an order or a goods received note. You raise this issue with your accounts supervisor. His response is to say 'don't worry, I'll authorise those for payment.'

You decide to investigate further and realise that this has happened on a number of previous occasions and always involved the same two suppliers invoices being authorised by the accounts supervisor. You suspect that the accounts supervisor may be in some way involved in defrauding the company.

What action should you take in this situation?

4.2* You work in the payroll department of Prestige Services Ltd, and one of your responsibilities is for the payment of staff expenses. You notice that a particular member of the sales staff makes substantially larger claims than any of his colleagues. When you investigate further you discover that he has been systematically over-claiming on his expenses since his employment with the organisation and you estimate that the total amount over-claimed is currently at least £4,000.

You raise this issue with your payroll supervisor who says that many members of staff 'fiddle' their expenses, and so she takes little notice of what you tell her.

What action should you take in these circumstances?

4.3* One of your roles as accounts supervisor for Splendid Ltd is to maintain the fixed asset register. On 1 March the company takes delivery of three brand new sports cars. When you ask for some more details about these cars you are told by the directors that they are actually for their own personal use, but should be treated as company cars in Splendid's accounts and should not be disclosed to the tax authorities as a taxable benefit for the directors.

You know that this is illegal as these cars are clearly provided for the directors' private use.

What action should you take in this situation?

4.4* You have recently been employed as an accounts supervisor at Dodgy Ltd. During the first few weeks of your employment you have become increasingly concerned about the way in which the company conducts its business. The following points have caused you particular concern:

(a) Sales made for cash are not always accounted for through the business. You know that the directors take some of the cash for their own personal expenditure.

(b) The business regularly employs casual staff in its warehouse without including them on the payroll. They are paid in cash.

(c) The casual staff detailed in (b) above are regularly handling toxic substances without appropriate protective clothing. These substances are known to affect long-term health.

What two main options are available to you in this situation?

4.5 You are employed as an accounts assistant for Bushfires, a large electrical manufacturer. The financial year end is approaching and the Financial Controller has asked you to assist him with the year end stock-take. Whist counting the stock the Production Manager explains to you that a significant number of the current stock of finished electric heaters are faulty. However, he goes on to explain that the faults 'are not too serious' and he intends to sell them off as good stock.

What should you do in this situation?

4.6 You are employed as the Finance Manager for a firm of solicitors and have a team of three more junior members who report to you. One of your staff has recently qualified and at his annual development review has indicated that he would like to take on some more responsibility. He has asked whether he could carry out the monthly billing for the firm.

As his manager should you hand over responsibility for the monthly billing to your junior colleague? Give reasons for your decision.

If you decide that he can take on this work what steps should you take to ensure that the work continues to be carried out to the required standard?

4.7 You work as one of the assistant accountants in the finance department of a large manufacturing company. The Finance Manager who you report to has asked you to prepare a schedule of repair and renewals as part of the preparation of the year-end accounts. After reviewing your completed schedule the Finance Manager calls you into his office and tells you that a number of the items on the schedule are incorrect and should have been capitalised rather than treated as replacement (renewal) costs.

When you try to explain why you included these items in the schedule the Finance Manager says 'I am too busy and what I say is final!'

Has your manager dealt with this situation correctly? If not, how should he have dealt with it?

4.8 You have recently been taken on as an accounts supervisor at Blackwell Ltd. On your curriculum vitae (CV) you stated that you have excellent skills and expertise over a wide range of computerised accounting packages. Although you are very familiar with the computer package that Blackwell uses, you have never used the management accounts functions. Your new manager has told you that as part of your role within the business you will be expected to prepare the monthly management accounts.

What steps should you take before taking on the responsibility for preparing the management accounts?

This chapter and the following two chapters of this book focus on the guidance on professional ethics given by the AAT to its members in practice – ie members who work for themselves or in firms, providing accountancy services to clients.

This chapter covers:

■ the need for independence when carrying out financial reporting and when acting in similar roles

■ situations where accountants act as agents for other organisations – eg for building societies

■ situations where accountants are offered commission payments

■ activities incompatible with the practice of public accountancy – running up gambling debts, for example

■ dealing with money held on behalf of clients

PERFORMANCE CRITERIA COVERED

unit 32: PROFESSIONAL ETHICS

Element 32.3:

develop, maintain and apply ethics in public practice

B   Identify and explain how specific situations can undermine professional independence.

C   Prepare a policy to be followed for handling client money.

D   Maintain independence and objectivity and impartiality in a range of circumstances.

MEMBERS IN PRACTICE

The term 'members in practice' refers to members of the AAT who work for themselves providing accounting and/or accounting related services to clients. They can be 'one person' practices or partners in a firm. In both these cases they are strictly speaking 'self-employed' members.

what members in practice should do

Section 5.1.1 of the Guidelines states that members who provide accounting, taxation or consultancy services in public practice must register on the AAT's scheme for members. They must also comply with the AAT Guidelines and Regulations for members in practice and the AAT's Guidelines on Professional Ethics.

what members in practice should not do

Section 5.1.2 explains a number of functions that members of the AAT are not permitted to carry out. You are **not** expected to remember these, but they are listed briefly below, as they are of interest:

- **external audit** (ie the audit of a UK limited company as required by the Companies Act or the audit of another body which requires the services of a registered auditor)

- undertake **investment business** or provide **corporate finance advice** to clients (ie activities subject to the Financial Services Act 1986)

- **insolvency work** (ie act as an insolvency practitioner in accordance with the provisions of the Insolvency Act 1986)

Members of the AAT **are**, however, permitted to work as part of a team providing these services provided they are working for a suitably qualified accountant, eg ICAEW, ACCA.

INDEPENDENCE

the importance of independence

One of the fundamental principles that we looked at in Chapter 1 was **objectivity** which we then explored in more detail in Chapter 2 when we considered the need for an accountant to be independent both in mind and in appearance (see pages 21-22). The Guidelines state (Section 5.2.1):

'When undertaking a financial reporting assignment, a member in practice should be independent both in fact and appearance.'

threats to independence

There are a number of potential threats to the independence of an AAT member in practice which are identified in section 5.2.4 of the Guidelines and summarised in the diagram below.

In the text that follows we will look at each of these types of threat in turn and identify situations where a member could be faced with a potential problem with his/her independence and objectivity.

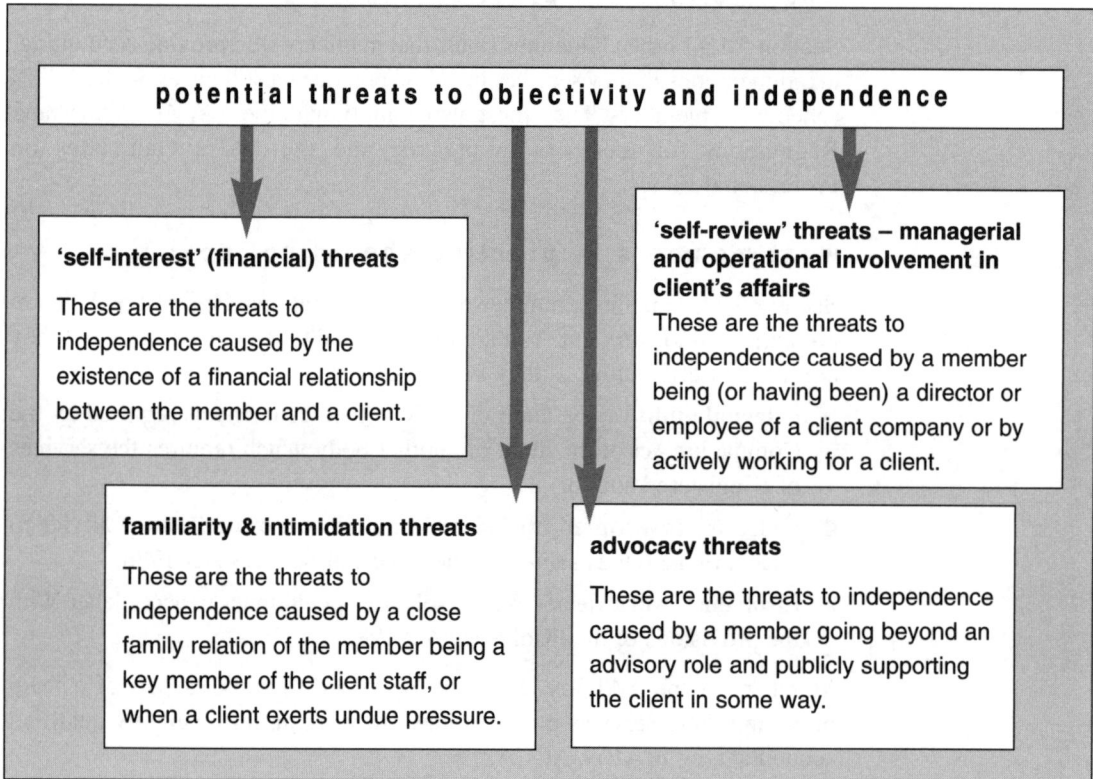

---

potential threats to objectivity and independence

'self-interest' (financial) threats

These are the threats to independence caused by the existence of a financial relationship between the member and a client.

'self-review' threats – managerial and operational involvement in client's affairs

These are the threats to independence caused by a member being (or having been) a director or employee of a client company or by actively working for a client.

familiarity & intimidation threats

These are the threats to independence caused by a close family relation of the member being a key member of the client staff, or when a client exerts undue pressure.

advocacy threats

These are the threats to independence caused by a member going beyond an advisory role and publicly supporting the client in some way.

---

self-interest (financial) threats to independence

Where a member in practice has a financial involvement with a client or in the affairs of a client, Section 5.2.6 states that this *'creates a self-interest threat to objectivity which is generally regarded as insurmountable'*.

There are four main areas where a financial involvement with a client can arise. They are:

■ direct or indirect financial interest

■ loans to or from the client or any officer, director or principal shareholder of a client company

■ holding a financial interest in a joint venture with a client or employee(s) of a client

■ when the receipt of fees from a client or group of connected clients represents a large proportion of the total gross fees of a member or the practice as a whole

We will now explain these areas of financial involvement in more detail.

direct or indirect financial interest in a client

If the member is a shareholder in a client company he/she would be considered to have a direct financial interest in that client. In this case the member's independence would be threatened as he/she would have a financial interest in the performance of the client business which could affect his/her judgement when preparing accounts or providing financial or tax advice. This self-interest threat would also extend to shares in a client held by a close relative of the member; for example the member's husband or wife.

The following example illustrates a situation of a self-interest threat resulting from a financial interest in a client.

example

shares in a client

Julie Parker acts as a self-employed accountant for a number of local firms. Her husband Simon and his business partner are considering buying shares in a local business and have been considering investing in one of Julie's clients, Doors & Windows Ltd. Simon discusses this proposal with Julie over dinner one evening.

What points should Julie raise with Simon?

If Simon and his partner were to buy shares in Doors & Windows this would create a self-interest threat to Julie's independence. The financial success of the company would have a direct impact on the value of the shares that Simon and his partner held. This in turn would affect the financial position of Julie and her husband.

Julie should explain to Simon that this would be a threat to her independence. In this situation Julie and Simon have two choices: either Simon can go ahead with his partner and buy the shares, in which case Julie should resign as accountant for Doors & Windows Ltd. Alternatively Simon should not go ahead with the planned purchase of shares in Doors & Windows Ltd.

loans to or from the client

If a client made a loan to a member who provided the client with accounting, taxation or other services, this could again affect the independence of the member. In this situation the client has financial influence over the member because of the money that is owed.

The example below illustrates a situation where this form of self-interest threat may arise.

---

example

loan from a client

Peter Moss is a member of the AAT and runs a small but successful accounting practice. Peter is keen to expand the firm, and during an informal chat with one of his clients, he explains that he is considering moving to larger premises and employing more staff. He also explains that he will need to arrange a substantial loan with the bank to allow him to do this. A few days later the client telephones Peter and states that he would be willing to lend Peter the money to finance his proposed business expansion.

Should Peter accept the offer?

Peter should not accept the offer of a loan from his client. This would immediately create a self-interest threat to Peter's independence through a financial involvement with the client. Peter should thank his client for the offer of the loan and politely say 'no, thanks'.

The only other solution would be for Peter to say to the client that he is no longer able to act as his accountant – but this is hardly realistic.

---

financial interest in a joint venture with the client

A self-interest threat would also arise for a member if he/she were to enter into a joint venture with a client or with an employee of the client. For reasons similar to those highlighted above, there would be a financial relationship between the client and the member which could compromise the independence of the member. We return to the example of the accountant Peter Moss to show how this threat could occur in practice.

---

example

the threat of a joint venture

A few days after Peter declined the loan from the client explained in the example above, he receives a further telephone call from the same client. The client says that he has been thinking about what Peter has said and believes he has a solution where he could help Peter with his business expansion without providing him with a loan. His suggestion is that he and Peter's firm embark on a joint venture to purchase the premises. Peter's firm would continue to provide accountancy services to existing and new clients. In return for his investment the client would expect a share of Peter's profits but would not be lending any money to Peter.

Should Peter now accept the offer given that the circumstances have changed?

Despite the changes in the nature of the offer, the client would still have a financial interest in Peter's firm and consequently there would be a self-interest threat to Peter's independence and so the offer should be politely refused. The only other solution, as before, is for Peter to resign as accountant for the client.

substantial fee income from a single client

If the fees that a member receives from an individual client represent a large percentage of the total gross fee income for the member (or the member's practice) this could again cause a self-interest threat to the member's independence. As the fee income from the client is so significant in relation to the member's total fee income this may well mean that the member cannot afford to lose the client which in turn could mean that the client has significant influence over the member.

example

the threat of substantial fee income

Sanjay Patel is a member of the AAT and runs a successful practice providing accountancy and taxation services to around 150 clients. His largest client, Emerson Ltd currently accounts for about 9% of his total fee income. Although Sanjay currently provides only accounting services to Emerson Ltd, the Managing Director of Emerson has asked whether he would like to take on the taxation work for the business. Sanjay estimates that the increased fees that this would generate would mean that Emerson Ltd would account for approximately 20% of his total fee income.

Should Sanjay provide the additional taxation services to Emerson Ltd?

The total fee income from Emerson Ltd if Sanjay were to take on the taxation work would represent a substantial proportion of Sanjay's total fee income. This could represent a self-interest threat to Sanjay's independence as Sanjay could become economically reliant on Emerson Ltd. Therefore in these circumstances Sanjay should not accept the additional work that Emerson is offering him.

self-review threats to independence – working for clients

Section 5.2.7 of the Guidelines, states that:

'When a member who is in practice is or was, within a period of two years prior to a potential assignment:

(i)   a member of the Board, an officer or employee of a company; or

(ii)   a partner of, or in the employment of, a member of the Board, or an officer or employee of the company;

then the member would be regarded as being subject to an insurmountable threat of a self-review nature, which would be incompatible with his or her continuing with a financial reporting assignment in relation to the company.'

This basically means that a member of the AAT is unable to take on the financial reporting for a company if he/she has recently had an active role in running that company. The member is also unable to take on the work where the same situation applies to a close family member or colleague.

This self-review threat to independence is illustrated in the following example.

---

example

an insurmountable 'self-review' threat

Iris McDonald is a qualified member of the AAT. She worked for a number of years as Finance Manager for Catchett and Rank Ltd, a company that designs computer games.

After leaving the company Iris was employed as a senior manager by Michael Croft & Co, a local firm of accountants. A year after joining, Iris became a full partner in the firm.

Shortly after this she received a telephone call from a director of her previous employer, Catchett and Rank Ltd. He congratulated her on becoming a partner and explained that they were looking for some new tax advisors and thought that Michael Croft & Co might be a good choice.

Should Iris agree on behalf of Michael Croft & Co to accept the assignment?

The Guidelines clearly state that where a member has been an employee of a potential client at any time in the previous two years this automatically threatens the independence of that member – it is what the Guidelines term an 'insurmountable threat'. Therefore, Iris should decline the offer from the director of Catchett and Rank.

providing other services for clients

The Guidelines also state (Section 5.2.8) that where members provide **consultancy services** to clients – eg management consultancy and tax advice – they must take care that they:

- make recommendations
- do **not** make management decisions
- do **not** take responsibility for management decisions

They should also avoid reporting on management decisions which they have recommended. Members should be independent advisors and not managers.

familiarity threat to independence

Where a member of the AAT has a family relationship with the client or a key member of the client staff, this relationship is seen by the Guidelines as having a negative effect on the objectivity and the independence of the member. Section 5.2.9 states that:

'There is a particular need to ensure that an objective approach to any assignment is not endangered as a consequence of any personal or family relationship.'

The following example highlights a situation where such a relationship exists and the effect it could have on the independence of an accountant.

example

the threat of a family relationship

Liz Robinson is a member of the AAT who owns and runs a small firm of accountants together with her business partner Tom Crusoe. She shares a house with her sister Jo who runs a successful training company. Up until now Jo has managed her own financial affairs, but her business is rapidly expanding and she can no longer manage the books herself. In addition, she has recently taken out a substantial business loan from her bank and, as part of the agreement, they have requested regular independently prepared financial statements.

Jo asks Liz if she will take on her business as a client. Should Liz accept this assignment?

There is a close family relationship between the two sisters which is made even closer by the fact that they share a house together. This close family relationship constitutes a familiarity threat to Liz's independence; consequently Liz should not agree to Jo's request and should instead recommend an alternative accountant to her sister.

intimidation threat to independence

If an accountant takes on a client and a relationship develops in which the accountant is 'bullied' or put under pressure by the client – 'intimidated' in other words – then the independence of the accountant is under threat in a very real sense. As a result the accountant's reporting could be biased in favour of the client. In cases such as these, the accountant should be changed. If a larger firm is involved, a stronger personality could be brought into the accountancy team to counter the client's threat to its independence.

advocacy threat to independence

Advocacy means that you are seen to support the client's point of view publicly – even in a court of law.

In the context of a threat to the independence of a member the advocacy threat is that the member could go beyond the **advisory** role that he/she should take for the client and **actively speak** on the client's behalf or in support of the client.

The Guidelines describe (Section 5.2.4) an advocacy threat as *'taking a strongly proactive stance on the client's behalf'*.

The threat that this situation could pose is illustrated in the following example.

example

an advocacy threat to independence

Hugh Davies is a qualified member of the AAT who provides a number of services to his clients, including accountancy services, management consultancy and taxation advice. Over the past few months Hugh has been providing management consultancy services to Naturally Green, a company that sells organic and environmentally friendly products.

The directors of Naturally Green are in the process of updating their marketing brochures and have asked Hugh to provide a written statement, as management consultant, endorsing the product range that they sell.

Should Hugh agree to provide the requested endorsement?

If Hugh were to provide an endorsement of Naturally Green's products he would be going beyond his advisory role for the client and would be 'taking a strongly proactive stance on the client's behalf'. This would have a seriously negative effect on Hugh's independence.

Consequently Hugh should refuse to provide the endorsement and should explain to the directors of Naturally Green the reasons for his refusal.

CONFLICT BETWEEN INTERESTS OF DIFFERENT CLIENTS

In Chapter 1 we discussed the issue of **conflict of interest** in relation to the objectivity of an accountant, explaining that members should not allow business or personal interests to prevent them from remaining objective and independent. The interests here are clearly those of the **accountant**.

In Section 5.2.10, the Guidelines explain how a conflict of interest can relate instead to the interests of the member's **clients**. Members who work in public practice normally have a significant number of different clients. Consequently there is a strong chance that at some point there may be a conflict of interest between two, or more, of these clients. For example the member may have a number of clients which work in the same market sector, all competing for the same customers, so the success of one client in increasing sales may well have a negative effect on another client in the same sector.

Section 5.2.10 states:

'There is, on the face of it, nothing improper in a member or practice having two or more clients whose interest may be in conflict'. In such a case however the work should be managed so as to avoid the interest of one client adversely affecting that of another.'

The issues for the member or practice working for clients where a potential conflict of interest exists are predominantly those of independence and confidentiality.

There are two potential problems which may face the member:

- the member may provide services and give professional advice to one client where he/she knows that this will have an adverse affect on another of his/her clients (independence).
- information gained about one client could potentially be beneficial to another and vice versa (confidentiality).

In many cases, the risk associated with these issues can be reduced to an acceptable level by compartmentalising the responsibilities and knowledge about each of the clients by using different members of staff to work on the client assignments. However, if this safeguard does not reduce the risk sufficiently then the member should not accept or continue one or more of the appointments.

When a member is considering taking on a new client or where there are any changes in the circumstances of existing clients the member should take all reasonable steps to find out whether a conflict of interests exists or could arise.

If a significant conflict of interest is identified between clients, the member should ensure that the clients involved are fully informed of the circumstances. This will then allow each of them to make an informed decision about whether to use the member's services.

The issue of conflict between the interests of different clients is illustrated in the example that follows.

example

a conflict of interest

Jim Kirk is an AAT member who runs Kirk & Co. a successful firm of accountants in Pineridge. Jim has recently been approached by Robert Redpool, one of the partners in Blackwell & Redpool, a local firm of builders asking if Kirk & Co. would be interested in carrying out some accounting and taxation work for them. One of Jim's existing clients, Bluebell & Whitelake is also a building firm located in Pineridge.

What points should Jim consider when deciding whether to accept the assignment for Blackwell & Redpool?

First, Jim must investigate whether there could be a conflict of interest between the potential client and his existing client, Bluebell & Whitelake. If he believes that there is, or could be, a conflict of interest between the two clients, Jim must then decide whether Kirk and Co have sufficient staff to use separate staff on each of the clients. This would reduce the risk that the interests of either client could be adversely affected if Kirk & Co took on the new work.

If Jim believes that he can adequately safeguard the interests of both clients he should then contact Blackwell & Redpool and Bluebell & Whitelake and fully explain the situation, including the staffing measures Kirk & Co intends to put in place. This will then allow the existing client and the potential client to decide for themselves whether they are happy to enter into, or continue in, a relationship with Kirk & Co.

If Jim decided that he could not sufficiently reduce the risks associated with the conflict of interest between the two builders, then he must either decline the appointment with Blackwell & Redpool (the more likely option) or end Kirk & Co.'s relationship with Bluebell & Whitelake.

SAFEGUARDS AGAINST THREATS TO INDEPENDENCE

How does a member in public practice ensure that his/her independence and objectivity are maintained when accepting or continuing to work for a client? How does a member deal with threats to that independence?

Section 5.2.5 of the Guidelines lists a number of possible safeguards and procedures that a member could put in place to help reduce the threats to a self-employed member's independence. These are in addition to any requirements provided for by law or by professional rules – for example the rules that govern the accountancy profession. The suggested safeguards are listed below. Read them through because they help to summarise much of what has been explained in this chapter so far.

- the need for an educational and experience requirement (eg the AAT qualifications) for entry into the profession

- continued training within the profession

- internal policies and procedures intended to promote quality control when dealing with clients and reporting on clients

- ongoing reviews of a firm's quality control systems

- arrangements to ensure that staff know about threats to independence and objectivity and can report any problems that relate to them

- a senior member of staff ('principal'), ideally a partner, who has not been involved in the day-to-day running of the assignment, should be actively involved, particularly in the final stage, to ensure that the objectivity of the firm is maintained

- consulting a third party such as a committee of independent directors, or a professional regulatory body (eg the AAT) in the case of any problems

- separating the responsibilities on an assignment to help reduce the potential risks to independence that can sometimes arise – for example, ensuring that staff involved in preparing the accounts for a client are separate from those giving taxation advice will help to maintain the overall independence of the members involved

- the threat to independence will be reduced if the senior members of staff involved in a professional assignment are rotated (changed round) regularly, eg from year-to-year

- in situations where external observers may believe that the independence of the firm could be compromised, the firm should consider making a public announcement, stating the way in which it will minimise this risk

- if a firm cannot find any other way to sufficiently reduce or remove a potential threat to its independence then it should refuse to carry out the assignment involved

AGENCIES

Until relatively recently it was fairly common in small towns in the UK for building societies to be represented by agents rather than opening full branches. These agencies were regularly operated by firms of accountants and allowed savers to deposit money into their building society accounts.

This has now become much less common since the Criminal Justice Act 1993 made money laundering illegal and required members to report any suspicions that they had to the National Criminal Intelligence Service. (Money laundering is covered in more detail on pages 121-123).

Because building society agencies predominantly accept deposits from personal customers, accountants are now faced with the risk of prosecution if they fail to investigate adequately the source of money that they accept from building society customers.

In addition, members who are agents for a building society are only permitted to accept deposits. They are not allowed to provide any of the other services normally associated with a building society, including investments, insurance and mortgage advice, unless they are authorised under the Financial Services Act 1986. By displaying a building society sign and offering building society leaflets there is a real danger that the public may perceive that the accountant is actually offering some of these additional services.

Taking these points into consideration, in normal circumstances, it would be inappropriate for a member to act as an agent for a building society or other organisation.

COMMISSION

Sometimes a member of the AAT may receive commission or some other type of reward when he/she introduces a client to another organisation. For example, a member may receive an introductory fee from a bank or insurance company for introducing a client who subsequently opens an account or takes out an insurance policy. In these cases the client is in a position where he/she has trust and confidence in the accountant's advice – because sound advice is what he/she has come to expect. The arrangement here is that *'the member will be accountable for the commission or reward to the client'*. (Guidelines, Section 5.4).

This means that where the role of the accountant involves representing the client or giving the client advice then the accountant must tell the client about the commission that he/she has been given for introducing them to another organisation. Under UK law the accountant is then obliged to pass over this commission or reward to the client, unless the client agrees that the member can keep it.

An example of where this could happen in practice now follows.

---

example

commission for an introduction

Jake Goody, a member in public practice, has been preparing the accounts for Big Sister Ltd for a number of years and has a very good working relationship with the directors of the company. With the increased exporting that Big Sister now undertakes, the directors have decided that the company should take out credit insurance on their debtors ledger. One of the directors has asked Jake to find a suitable insurer and arrange an introductory meeting.

After researching potential insurers Jake decides to recommend McCalls as a suitable insurer. When he contacts McCalls they explain that it is their policy to pay a commission to the introducer where a new policy is taken out.

What action must Jake take with regard to this commission payment?

If Big Sister decides to take out an insurance policy with McCalls, Jake must ensure that he fully discloses the introductory commission to the directors of Big Sister. He must also explain that he is legally obliged to pass over this commission to Big Sister whilst also pointing out that they can if they wish agree that he can keep it as a legitimate payment for the work that he has carried out.

INCOMPATIBLE ACTIVITIES

Most public accountancy practices will provide one, or more, of the following services to their clients:

- accounting
- auditing
- taxation
- management consultancy
- financial management

However, there may be situations where a member is also involved in another business, occupation or activity that may be unrelated to public accountancy services. In this case the accountant must ensure that this activity does not affect his/her ability to conduct professional business in accordance with the fundamental ethical principles of the accountancy profession.

The issue of incompatible activities is covered in Section 5.7.1 of the Guidelines.

'Members in public practice should not concurrently engage in any business, occupation or activity which impairs or might impair their integrity, objectivity or independence, or the good reputation of the profession, and therefore would be incompatible with the rendering of public accountancy services.'

The key point here is that a member of the AAT who works in public practice should not also be involved in any activity that will affect his/her integrity, objectivity or independence or will bring the good reputation of the accountancy profession into disrepute.

So what sort of activities would potentially fall into the category of 'incompatible activities'?

Here are some examples together with the reasons for their inclusion:

- a member who runs up significant gambling debts with a client organisation – the fact that the member owes the client money could impair his/her independence
- a member who consistently pays his/her own bills far beyond the due date – this could bring into question the integrity of the member
- a member who overcharges clients for the work that he/she performs – again whilst this is not illegal it would be considered unethical and reflect badly on the member's integrity
- a member who is generally sloppy in his/her work and does not take sufficient care over the assignments that he/she completes – this will reflect badly on the accounting profession and again questions the member's integrity
- a member who is an active campaigner for animal rights, including being involved in demonstrations and potentially illegal activities – this may not be appropriate for the maintenance of the good reputation of the accounting profession
- a member who represents an openly racist political party in local council elections – again this could bring the accounting profession into disrepute

A member of the AAT should be able to use his/her own professional judgement as to whether an activity that he/she is or potentially may become involved in could threaten his/her integrity or could bring the good reputation of the accountancy profession into disrepute. However, if the member has any doubt he/she should seek advice from the AAT using the AAT Ethics Advice Line.

CLIENTS' MONIES

Members of the AAT who work in public practice may sometimes hold money ('monies') that belongs to their clients. This could be as a result of a direct request from the client or could be during the course of the services they are providing to the client.

In all circumstances where an accountant is holding client monies there are strict rules and procedures that must be followed.

financial services and money laundering

There are two pieces of legislation that govern the holding of client monies by a member of the AAT working in public practice. First, under the terms of the **Financial Services Act 1986** members operating in the UK cannot hold clients' monies for investment business unless they have been authorised to do so. In reality it is unlikely that this would be something a member would actually become involved in.

Under the terms of the **Criminal Justice Act 1993** together with the Money Laundering regulations a member should not hold client monies if there is reason to believe that they were obtained from, or are to be used for, illegal activities. If a member is not able to ascertain where the money has come from he/she should not hold the monies for the client.

procedures for holding client money

Section 5.8 of the Guidelines details a number of procedures that must be followed where a member holds client monies. These procedures are summarised below and illustrated by the example that follows.

■ client monies should be kept separately from personal monies or monies belonging to the practice

■ client monies should only be used for the purpose for which they are intended

■ a member in public practice should always be ready to account for client monies to any person entitled to such accounting

■ one or more bank accounts should be maintained for client monies

■ when opening a bank account for client monies a member should give written notice to the bank stating the title and nature of the account and requiring acknowledgement in writing from the bank that they accept the terms of the notice

■ all client monies received by a member should be deposited without delay

■ monies should only be withdrawn from a client account on the instructions of the client or for the client's benefit

■ the client's account should never go overdrawn

■ where the client's money is likely to remain in the account for more than two months, and the balance is over £2,000, the money should with the agreement of the client, be placed in an interest-bearing account

■ all interest earned on client monies should be credited to the client

■ members should keep sufficient books and records clearly detailing how they have dealt with client monies both generally and in relation to specific clients

■ a statement of account should be provided to clients at least once a year

The following example illustrates how these points would work in practice.

example

handling client monies

Emma Edgar runs a successful firm of accountants and tax advisors. As part of the tax services that Emma's firm provide they often hold money on deposit for their clients until the due date for payment of tax to HMRC. Although some firms will have only one account for client monies, it is this firm's policy to set up individual accounts for each client. Giles, a new member of staff, is unclear what to do when a new client asks him to hold £3,400 until the tax is due for payment.

What should Emma tell Giles to do?

Giles should first ascertain that the money has come from a legitimate source. Provided that he is satisfied, he must then write to the bank giving notice that an account should be set up in the client's name for the purpose of holding money for tax payments until the due date and requesting written acknowledgement of his request. If the money is likely to remain in the account for more than two months he should ensure that the bank pays interest on the balance.

When the account has been set up and the money paid in, Giles must ensure any further money is paid in without delay and that withdrawals are only made on instruction from the client. The account should also never go overdrawn. Clear and accurate books and records must be kept for the account and a statement provided to the client at least annually.

payment of fees

The Guidelines (Section 5.8.8) also deal with the question of client monies held and the payment of fees charged by accountants. They basically state that a member cannot decide to use money that they are holding for a client to pay themselves fees owed by the client – unless this has been specifically arranged with the client, or more than thirty days have passed since the member first billed the client.

<table>
<tr><td>

Chapter Summary

</td><td>

- There are certain functions that members of the AAT are not permitted to undertake, these include external audits, investment business or advice and insolvency work.

- Members of the AAT who work in public practice must be independent both in fact and appearance.

- There are four main threats to the independence of a member working in public practice which are self-interest threats, self-review threats, familiarity threats and advocacy threats.

- The Guidelines detail a number of safeguards that members are able to put in place to minimise or negate these threats.

- Where a conflict of interest exists between two or more clients a member should take all possible steps to minimise the risks that could arise.

- Members who act as agents (eg as building society agents) should limit their duties to accepting client deposits unless authorised to do further activities under the Financial Services Act 1986.

- Where a member receives commission for introducing a client to another organisation he/she should give this to the client unless the client specifically says that the member can keep it.

- Members of the AAT should not engage in any business, occupation or activity which could impair their integrity, objectivity or independence, or which would bring the good reputation of the accountancy profession into disrepute.

- When holding client monies members should ensure that they have fully ascertained where the monies have come from.

- The Guidelines detail strict procedures that a member must follow when holding client monies.

</td></tr>
</table>

Key Terms	**self-interest threat to independence**	the threat caused by a financial relationship between the member and a client
	self-review threats to independence	the threat caused by a member currently or recently being a director or an employee of a client company or by actively working for a client
	familiarity threats to independence	the threat caused by a close family relation of the member being a key member of the client staff
	intimidation threats to independence	the threat caused by a client exerting undue pressure on a member
	advocacy threats to independence	the threat caused by a member going beyond an advisory role and publicly supporting the client in some way
	agencies	the situation where firms of accountants working in public practice operate as agents on behalf of building societies or other organisations
	commission	a financial payment made to a member for introducing a client to another organisation as a customer
	client monies	money that belongs to a client and which the member is holding on the client's behalf while acting on the client's behalf

Student Activities

answers to the asterisked (*) questions are to be found at the back of this book.

5.1* Simon Lewis has been operating as an accountant in public practice for a number of years employing eight members of staff and providing services to around 120 clients. His firm's annual fee income is approximately £700,000.

Simon has recently been approached by a very large potential new client who is interested in using Simon's firm to prepare annual accounts and tax returns. Simon's firm has no clients that are anywhere near the size of this potential new client. Simon estimates that the fee income from this client would be £230,000.

Should Simon take on this new client? Explain the reasoning behind your answer.

5.2* You have been working for the past six months for George Broom & Son, a firm of accountants. The senior partner, Jeff Broom, has recently received an enquiry from Cartwright & Sands a local firm of chartered surveyors. Jeff was not involved in your recruitment and only met you briefly after your final interview with another of the partners. He is, therefore, unaware that before coming to work for George Broom & Son you were employed as Financial Controller at Cartwright & Sands.

At the weekly staff meeting Jeff explains that he is currently in discussion with Cartwright & Sands to take on the preparation of their year-end accounts.

What action should you take in this situation? Explain why you would take this action.

5.3* Maurice Leblanc is a member of the AAT who is one of the three partners in a medium-sized accountancy practice. He has recently set up home with his girlfriend Anne-Marie who runs a successful hairdressing business.

Anne-Marie has asked Maurice if his firm could take on her hairdressing business as a client because she no longer wishes to complete the accounting records herself.

Discuss the reasons why Maurice should/should not accept this assignment.

5.4* Maddie Morris is a qualified member of the AAT who provides a number of services to her clients, including accountancy services, management consultancy and taxation advice. Connor & Jackson, one of Maddie's clients for whom she prepares accounts, is currently looking for new investors in their business and has asked Maddie to attend a meeting with a potential investor and to speak on their behalf.

What ethical points should Maddie consider before agreeing to the request from Connor & Jackson?

5.5   Lisa Greer is a member of the AAT and is the senior partner in Greer & Co, a medium-sized firm of accountants in Beechwood. Lisa receives a call from Gerry Preen a successful local printing firm asking if Greer & Co. would be interested in becoming his accountants and preparing his year-end accounts.

One of Lisa's existing clients, Oscar Townsend runs the only other printers in Beechwood.

What ethical points should Lisa consider when deciding whether to accept the assignment for Gerry Preen?

5.6   You are a member of the AAT who works for Sintons, a firm of accountants in public practice. Johnston & Beecham, one of the firm's larger clients, has recently decided that it should now take out professional indemnity insurance and has asked you to research possible insurers and arrange introductory meetings with two or three appropriate insurers.

After researching potential options you decide that there are two potential insurers who best suit your client's needs. You arrange meetings between each of these insurers and Johnston & Beecham which you also attend.

After these meetings your client decides to take out an insurance policy with one of the two insurers that you have recommended. Two weeks later you receive a cheque for £1,000 from the insurance company as an introductory commission.

What should you do with this commission payment? Explain the reasons for your decision.

5.7   You are a partner in a successful firm of accountants and are sometimes expected to hold money on deposit for your clients. In such circumstances your firm's policy is to set up individual accounts for each client. A new client asks you to hold £15,000 for him until he pays it to the vendor for a property that he is currently purchasing.

Describe the steps that you should take in this situation to ensure that you deal with the client's monies in accordance with the AAT Guidelines on Professional Ethics.

This chapter looks at the ethical guidance that the AAT gives to members in public practice when they are taking on new clients.

This chapter covers:

■ letters of engagement that are sent out to clients at the beginning of an assignment and which set out the responsibilities of the accountant and the client

■ the ways in which fees and commissions are calculated for the work that is carried out for clients

■ the procedures that should be followed when a client changes accountant

■ the way in which accountants can advertise their services to obtain professional work

■ the acceptable format for the names and letterheads of accountants in public practice

PERFORMANCE CRITERIA COVERED

unit 32: PROFESSIONAL ETHICS

Element 32.3

develop, maintain and apply ethics in public practice

A   Prepare appropriate letters of engagement and develop and implement a fair fees policy for your professional services.

D   Maintain independence and objectivity and impartiality in a range of circumstances.

E   Make recommendations for a policy statement in relation to a client wishing to change accountant.

G   Prepare clear guidelines which should be followed to advertise your accounting services in a professional and ethical manner.

LETTERS OF ENGAGEMENT

purpose of the letter of engagement

When a member in practice is employed by a client to carry out any form of accounting work, either on a 'one-off' or ongoing basis, it is normal for the accountant to issue a **letter of engagement**. This is a formal letter which provides written confirmation of:

- the extent of the work that is to be undertaken by the accountant

- the respective responsibilities of the accountant and the client

The letter is agreed and signed by both the accountant and the client.

contents of the letter of engagement

Section 5.5.1 of the Guidelines gives a list of what the AAT recommends should be included in a letter of engagement that a member in practice sends to a client. A summary of the points is listed below.

■ The letter of engagement should clearly set out the **nature and scope of the assignment**, ie whether it is accounting, taxation, consultancy or another type of service. Also if the member is going to produce a report at the end of the assignment, details should be given of the report's format.

■ The letter of engagement should set out an appropriate **timetable** for the assignment, including when the work is due to start, how long it is expected to take and when reports are due to be made. It should also include whether the work is a one-off assignment or on a recurring basis.

■ The letter of engagement should clearly set out the **responsibilities of the client**, for example the books and records that the accountant will need and when they will be needed.

■ The letter should state that it is the **client's responsibility to detect errors and fraud**, unless, of course, the client and the accountant have agreed that this responsibility is a specific part of the assignment.

■ The letter should contain details of how the accountant's **fees** are to be calculated, together with details of what action the accountant will take with regard to **unpaid fees**.

■ The letter of engagement should set out who owns the **books and records** that are created during the assignment, ie the accountant's files that are created. It will also show details of the accountant's

policy on keeping, destroying and returning documents. For example, if the accountant may have a policy of returning documents to the client as soon as the bill is paid, or destroying documents after a set period of time if the client does not request them.

■ If the accountant's work will be used by a **third party**, for example where the client uses the accounts to support a loan application, this must be specified in the letter of engagement and the accountants must make sure that they include a disclaimer that the information is provided only for client use and should not be shown to any other party without the accountants' prior consent

You should now study the sample letter of engagement which is shown in Appendix 2 (page 207).

FEES AND COMMISSIONS

providing a professional service

So far in this book we have discussed the ethical requirements that are expected of professional accountants and particularly AAT members. In other words, when carrying out work for their clients, members in public practice are expected to conform to technical accounting standards and to perform the work with integrity and objectivity.

Members of the accounting profession are able to carry out their work with these ethical requirements in mind because of the professional skills and knowledge that they have gained through their training and experience.

When accountants carry out assignments for their clients they are entitled to be paid for it – which comes as no surprise! We will now describe the ways in which accountants charge for the work that they do.

how fees are normally calculated

It is important when an accountant takes on an assignment for a client that both parties agree the basis on which the fees are going to be calculated. A summary of this should be set out in the letter of engagement.

Section 5.6.2 of the Guidelines suggests that a member should base his/her fees on the following factors:

■ the skills and knowledge needed for the work involved
■ the level of training and experience needed

- the time that will be needed to carry out the assignment
- the level of responsibility that the work entails

In practice, this means that accountants normally base their fees on an agreed rate per hour, or per day, for the different levels of staff involved on an assignment. This is illustrated in the example that follows.

example

a question of fees

Briers & Bramble, a firm of accountants has recently completed the year-end accounts for one of its clients, Penfold Ltd. Robert Briers has asked you to calculate the fees for this assignment and has provided you with the following information on the time taken:

- two Junior Trainees for eight days each
- one Senior for eight days
- one Manager for two days
- five hours of the Partner's time

Briers and Bramble's standard charge-out rates (excluding VAT) are as follows:

Junior Trainee	£175	per day
Senior	£280	per day
Manager	£500	per day
Partner	£120	per hour

How much should Penfold be charged?

The fees calculation for Penfold should be calculated by applying the standard charge-out rates to the number of hours or days that the assignment took at each level.

2 Junior Trainees for 8 days at £175/day		
= 2 x 8 x £175	=	£2,800
1 Senior for 8 days at £280/day		
= 8 x £280	=	£2,240
1 Manager for 2 days at £500/day		
= 2 x £500	=	£1,000
1 Partner for 5 hours at £120/hour		
= 5 x £120	=	£600
Total fees to be charged (excluding VAT)	=	£6,640

Note that in order to avoid any misunderstanding, it should be made clear whether the fees include or exclude VAT.

In the above example, the charge-out rates for different levels of staff increase as the seniority of the staff increases. This reflects the skills and knowledge and the experience of more senior staff and also the responsibility that they must take. The charge-out rate for a partner is the most expensive. This makes sense because the partner will be the most experienced member of staff and will take overall responsibility for the work that is carried out by his/her team.

quoting for new assignments

One of the key factors that will help a client decide whether or not to use a particular firm of accountants will be the fee that will be charged. It would be tempting for an accountant to provide a very low estimate for an assignment in order to improve the chances of getting the business. Section 5.6.6 of the Guidelines states that there is no reason why an accountant should not quote a lower fee than has been charged in a previous period provided it does not affect the quality of the work. However, in Section 5.6.4, the Guidelines specifically state that a member should not quote an estimated fee, which he/she knows will substantially increase once the work is carried out, without telling the client.

This example that follows shows how this could arise in practice.

example

how low can you go?

Warne & Panesar, a firm of accountants, have been asked to produce a quote for a possible new client. During a meeting the potential client tells one of the partners, Kiran Panesar, that in order to be selected for the job the fee that Warne & Panesar quote must be at least 20% less than they are paying their current accountants.

Kiran knows that the client's current bill is £16,000 and that a 20% reduction would mean that the quote would have to be £12,800. She also knows that according to Warne and Panesar's standard charge-out rates the assignment should be charged at approximately £14,500. She is very keen to get the work and is considering what the implications would be if she were to quote for the work at the lower figure of £12,800.

What should Kiran do in this situation?

Warne & Panesar can quote a fee lower than the client is currently paying provided that the quality of the work that they carry out does not suffer. Kiran will need to examine the estimate that she has prepared to see whether it is possible to reduce it in any way. However, given the large difference between £14,500 and £12,800, this would probably mean reducing the number of hours or the grade of staff used. This could adversely affect the quality of the work.

Kiran could quote £12,800 as an estimate for the work and then increase the fee at a later date when the actual work is carried out. However, Section 5.6.4 of the Guidelines specifically states that this is not acceptable practice.

Therefore the only realistic options open to Kiran are either:

1   quote at the lower fee of £12,800 and accept that the firm will make a reduced profit on the assignment.

or . . .

2   quote her original estimate of £14,500 for the assignment, explaining that this is nearly 10% less than the client is currently paying and that the work cannot be carried out to the required standard for a lower fee than this.

contingent fees

Sometimes a client may ask an accountant to undertake work where the fee will be paid on a **contingent** basis.

Contingent fees mean that the client will only have to pay the accountant if the work results in an agreed outcome.

Contingent fees, where the fee is only paid if a specified result is obtained, cannot be charged on financial reporting services such as the preparation of a client's tax returns. This is because it could create a self-interest threat to the accountant's objectivity. For example the situation where the accountant will only be paid if the client's tax bill is below an agreed amount could influence him/her to adjust the figures to achieve this result.

Where an accountant is asked to perform a non-financial reporting service for a client on a contingency basis the member must think very carefully about whether there is a self-interest threat to his/her independence before agreeing to carry out the work on this basis.

In the following example, contingency fees could be charged.

example

contingent fees

Johann Pfaff is a member of the AAT who works in public practice. One of his clients, Septimus Ltd has asked him to prepare a business plan to support a loan application to the bank. The Managing Director of Septimus Ltd has asked that Johann's fee should be dependent on the success or otherwise in getting the loan.

Should Johann accept the assignment on this basis?

The MD of Septimus Ltd is suggesting that Johann performs this work on a contingent fee basis. If the loan application is not successful Johann will not be paid by Septimus for this work. Provided Septimus does not ask Johann to give a professional opinion on the business plan there is no financial reporting involved in this work. There is therefore no reason why Johann should not perform the work on this basis, provided he is happy to accept the risk in doing so.

percentage fees

An accountant will sometimes carry out work for a client where the fee is calculated on a percentage basis. For example, this could be as a percentage of money saved or money recovered in legal disputes. Sometimes, in these cases, the client will not be able to pay the accountant's fees unless there is a successful outcome to the work involved. For example, a client may ask his/her accountant to carry out some debt recovery work. If no money is recovered from the debtors then no fees will be due because any percentage of £0 is £0. Fees that are charged on a percentage basis will normally be treated as contingent fees.

The next example shows how a percentage fee could be agreed in practice.

example

percentage fees

Raymond Noir is an accountant in practice. One of his clients, Predator Ltd is keen to take over another business, Target Ltd (which is not one of Raymond's clients) and has been quoted a purchase price of £220,000. The management of Predator Ltd believes that this is too expensive and has asked Raymond to carry out some analysis to assist them in their negotiations to reduce the price. They have told Raymond that if he accepts the work they will pay him 30% of any savings they make on the initial price of £220,000, but only if the purchase goes through.

Should Raymond accept the assignment on this basis?

The work that Raymond has been asked to do is not financial reporting and he does not have to give a professional opinion. Therefore, he can accept this assignment on a contingent fees basis as there is no requirement for him to be independent and hence there is no self-interest threat.

expenses

Expenses such as travelling to and from the client that are incurred by the accountant because he/she is carrying out a particular assignment will normally be charged back to the client in addition to professional fees. Details of these expenses should be included in the letter of engagement.

the need for clarity in explaining the fees structure

Now that we have examined the various ways in which an accountant can charge for work carried out, you will be able to appreciate the importance of setting out **very clearly** in the letter of engagement the basis of the calculation of fees to avoid any misunderstanding.

CHANGES IN PROFESSIONAL APPOINTMENT

changing accountants

From time to time clients will decide to change their accountants. Possible reasons for this could be because they are unhappy with the service they are currently getting or that they believe that they can get a cheaper or a better service elsewhere. Also, in certain instances, it will be the accountant who decides to resign from an assignment with a particular client.

Regardless of whose decision it is, when there is a change in accountant, it is very important that the prospective accountant and the existing accountant communicate with each other promptly. This will allow the new accountant to check whether there are any professional reasons why he/she cannot accept the appointment.

Most practices would normally have a defined policy that its staff should follow when accepting new clients which should include the points covered in this section.

We will now describe the way in which this communication between 'old and new' accountants takes place.

communicating with the previous accountant

Communication between prospective and existing accountants should allow the new accountants to make a responsible decision whether or not to accept an appointment with a new client. At this stage it is worth pointing out that this decision is wholly that of the new accountant – the existing accountant cannot decide whether to give permission for the new accountant to act.

So how does the change-over actually work in practice?

First, the new accountant should check to ensure that the client has informed their existing accountant of the proposed change and has given them permission to co-operate with the new accountant.

The new accountant should then write to the previous accountant to request **professional clearance** together with any other relevant information he/she might need to take over the assignment. As the phrase suggests, if an accountant gives 'professional clearance', it means that there are no professional reasons why the new accountant should not take on the assignment for the client. Ideally this confirmation should be in writing.

It is the professional responsibility of the existing accountant, who receives a request from a new accountant, to co-operate fully and answer promptly. He/she should tell the new accountant whether there are any issues that his/her proposed successor should know about – or confirm that no such issues exist.

A sample text of a professional clearance letter is shown below.

---

address

date

Dear Sirs

Name of client

We have been asked to act as accountant and tax advisor for the above client.

We are writing to enquire if you are aware of any professional reason why we should not take up this appointment.

If you are not aware of any reasons why we should not take up the appointment, we shall be grateful if you will kindly let us have the following information relating to the client:

1   accounts for the last financial year

2   trial balance for the last financial year

3   the most recent tax computations and tax return, as appropriate

4   any other information which would assist in the preparation of the accounts and tax computations

Yours faithfully

the decision to accept a new appointment

When the new accountant has received a reply from the existing accountant he/she must then decide:

■ whether to accept the appointment

■ if the issues that the existing accountant has raised need to be investigated further before accepting the assignment

■ whether to decline the assignment

There are a number of reasons why an accountant might decline an appointment. Section 5.9.9 of the AAT Guidelines specifically states that where an existing accountant's fees have not been paid by the client, this is not in itself a reason for the new accountant to refuse the assignment, although, of course, it could tip the balance towards a refusal of the assignment.

The next example highlights a situation where an accountant must decide whether or not to accept a new assignment.

example

accepting a new assignment

Mike Costas, an accountant who works in public practice, has been asked to act for a new client, Hexagon Homes. However, Hexagon Homes have specifically asked that he does not contact their existing accountants. They tell Mike that they will contact their existing accountants to obtain all the necessary information that he requires.

What should Mike do in this situation?

As part of the change in accountants for Hexagon Homes, Mike needs to obtain professional clearance from the existing accountants. The client's request not to contact the existing accountants means that this clearance cannot be obtained. Unless Mike can persuade Hexagon Homes to give permission for him to contact the existing accountant and for them to co-operate freely with him, then he should decline the assignment.

defamation

Defamation means: **'to damage someone or someone's reputation by saying or writing bad things about them which are not true'**

There may be circumstances where the information that an existing accountant communicates to the new accountant could be damaging to the client or other individuals associated with the client's business. Examples of this could include negative statements about the client's integrity or honesty, or may even relate to possible criminal acts carried out by the client.

Naturally, a client will not be happy if such information is passed on to the new accountant, particularly if they know that it is not true. In some cases this could lead the client to bring a legal action against the existing accountant for **defamation**.

If such a legal action is brought against an accountant he/she is likely to be protected by what is called '**qualified privilege**'. This means that the accountant should not have to pay damages to a client for defamatory statements provided the accountant has made these statements without deliberately wishing to harm or upset the client (ie maliciously).

A statement made by an accountant will not be viewed as malicious provided that he/she honestly believes it to be true and has avoided making reckless allegations against a client which he/she could have no reason to believe are true.

This point is illustrated by the example which follows.

example

a question of defamation

Jean Rook works in public practice and until recently has acted for a client Pawn & Castle. Jean has been concerned for a while about the fact that the directors of Pawn & Castle regularly take cash out of the business without accounting for it as drawings or salary. At a recent meeting there was a heated discussion between Jean and the Managing Director of Pawn & Castle which resulted in the client informing Jean that they intended to change accountants.

Two weeks after the meeting Jean received a letter from another firm of accountants, Bishop & Co., asking for professional clearance. She replies stating the concerns she has about the cash withdrawals from the business and providing all other necessary information that Bishop & Co have requested.

Three weeks later Jean receives notification of a legal action being brought against her by Pawn & Castle for defamation.

Is it likely that Pawn & Castle's action for damages against Jean will be successful?

Provided Jean can show that when she sent the letter of clearance to Bishop & Co she sincerely believed the statements she made were true, and there was no malicious intent, then it is unlikely that the action for damages by Pawn & Castle will be successful as Jean will be protected by 'qualified privilege'.

additional related work

A member of the accounting profession may be asked by a client to take on some work that is separate from work that is already being provided by another accountant. An example of this would be where a client takes on one accountant to prepare tax returns and asks a different accountant to prepare the accounting statements.

In these circumstances the member being asked to carry out the additional work should inform the existing accountant of the work that he/she has been asked to take on.

The client may provide good reasons why the new accountant should not inform the existing accountant of his/her appointment. If the new accountant accepts the assignment without having communicated with the previous accountant, he/she must be aware of the increased risk of later finding out information which would have affected his/her decision at that time.

OBTAINING PROFESSIONAL WORK

obtaining new work

There are a number of ways in which a member of the AAT working in public practice can obtain new work. They could be recommended by existing clients, by word of mouth or through advertising their services. In section 5.12 of the Guidelines the AAT give specific guidance on the appropriate ways in which a member can go about promoting his/her firm.

Members of the AAT must ensure that the way in which they advertise the services of their practice is consistent with the dignity of the accounting profession. This means the advertising should put across an image of a professional organisation that is committed to high ethical and technical standards.

legal and regulatory requirements on advertising

Any advertising must comply with the local law of the country where it takes place. In the UK it must also conform to the requirements of various advertising authorities including the British Code of Advertising Practice. This should particularly relate to legality, decency, clarity, honesty and truthfulness.

Accountants who are bound by the ethical code of conduct of their profession must ensure that they always comply with these legal and regulatory requirements.

advertising professional fees

One of the factors a new client will consider when deciding which accountant to use will be the fees that will have to be paid. It may, therefore, be tempting for the accountant to make his/her fees look as attractive as possible in advertising material.

Section 5.12.2 (iii) states the following about any reference made in advertising to fees:

'the greatest care should be taken to ensure that such reference does not mislead as to:

- *the precise services to be covered; and*

- *the basis of current and future fees'*

It is very important for an accountant to be very clear as to how his/her fees will be calculated and exactly what services the fees will cover. Consequently, accountants will often offer a free initial consultation to potential clients at which fees levels can be discussed in more detail.

example

advertising fees

Jayne Reynolds works for Arthur Bowen & Co, a firm of accountants. She is currently producing an advertisement to put in the local evening newspaper to attract new clients to the firm. She shows the draft advertisement to several other members of staff who make the following suggestions regarding the section on fees:

> 'Why don't we offer a free no-obligation introductory consultation to all new clients?'

> 'Why don't we offer all new clients a 15% discount for the first year?'

Should Jayne include these suggestions in the advertisement?

There is no problem with Arthur Bowen & Co offering a free introductory consultation. This may appeal to potential clients as it will give them an opportunity to ask any questions they have and to clarify the fees that they will be charged.

The issue with offering a percentage discount is on what basis the 15% will be calculated. Jayne must make it clear that the 15% will be calculated on the fees that would otherwise have been charged by Arthur Bowen & Co for the service.

comparisons with other practices

Another technique that accountants might adopt when advertising professional services is to compare their practices with those of other accountants. When a member or a practice chooses to make this kind of comparison in any of its promotional material, Section 5.12.2 (iv) of the Guidelines states:

'members should ensure that such comparisons:

- *are objective and not misleading*
- *relate to the same services*
- *are factual and verifiable, and*
- *do not discredit or denigrate the practice or services of others.'*

This means that if the member does decide to compare his/her practice with that of another accountant he/she must be totally unbiased and must be able to prove that what is being said is true. To **denigrate** another firm is to say that they are not good at what they do. Therefore a member must take care not to make any negative comments about another practice.

Members must take particular care about any claims that they make about the size or quality of their firms because such claims are very difficult to prove. For example, it is impossible to know whether a claim to be 'the largest firm' in an area is a reference to the number of partners or staff, the number of offices or the amount of fee income. Similarly a claim to be 'the best firm' is subjective and cannot be supported by any facts. Therefore, statements like this should not be included in advertising for members' practices.

We will now return to the example of Jayne Reynolds (see previous page) who is preparing an advertisement for Arthur Bowen & Co.

example

comparison with other practices

The staff at Arthur Bowen & Co have made some other suggestions for points that could be included in the advertisement. Jayne is now considering whether or not to include any of them. These suggestions are:

'We're very good at what we do so shouldn't we say that we are the best firm in the area?'

'As we've got four offices couldn't we say that we're the biggest firm in the area?'

'All our clients say how reasonable our fees are, can't we say that we're cheaper than other firms?'

Should Jayne include any of these suggestions in the advertisement?

A claim to be the best firm in the area is subjective, and relies on personal opinions rather than on facts. It is therefore difficult to prove and so should not be included in the advertisement.

The number of offices that a firm has could be one measure of the size of a firm; however, size could also be measured by the number of staff or by total fee income. Therefore, again this claim should be avoided.

Finally, if in its advertising Arthur Bowen & Co says that it is cheaper than other accountants, the firm must ensure that the comparison is not misleading and relates to the same services provided by other practices. It must also ensure that the claim is based on fact and can be proved and also that it does not discredit or denigrate any other practice.

We can see that members must be very careful before deciding to compare their services with those of other practices in their advertising. They must ensure that any claims that they make can be proved and that they do not make negative comments about other accountants.

harassment

Members must remember that it is the client's decision whether to employ an accountant to act for him/her. We have seen in the above sections that it is acceptable for a member to promote his/her services through advertising. However, members must not promote themselves in a way that could be seen as harassment of potential clients. **Harassment** means **'behaviour that annoys or upsets someone'.**

An accountant must not put pressure on a client by repeatedly contacting them either in person, by telephone or in writing as this could be viewed as harassment. If the potential client were to make a complaint of harassment against a member of the AAT it would normally be up to the member to demonstrate that any repeated approaches he/she made did not amount to harassment.

This point is illustrated below with an example based on the example of Jayne Reynolds who is preparing an advertisement for Arthur Bowen & Co.

example

following up on client interest

The advertisement for Arthur Bowen & Co generated much interest in their services and Jayne has held introductory meetings with six potential new clients. She asks one of the junior accountants, Robert Crewe, to follow up these meetings with a telephone call to find out whether there is any further information that they may need.

On Friday morning Jayne comes into the office to hear Robert on the telephone, saying:

'Hello again! This is Robert Crewe from Arthur Bowen & Co. Hope you got my other messages. Please could you give me a call to discuss whether you would like our practice to carry out any work for you?'

What should Jayne do in this situation?

Jayne clearly intended that Robert make brief courtesy calls to these prospective clients. He has obviously made a number of calls to this particular potential client which could be viewed as harassment, especially as they have not called him back.

Jayne should now talk to Robert to find out how many times he has telephoned this prospective client and how many messages he has left. She should also ask him whether he has done the same with any of the other potential clients. Having done this she should telephone the prospective client(s) herself and explain that it was not her intention for Robert's calls to put pressure on them and they were merely courtesy calls to find out if they needed any further information.

Finally Jayne should explain to Robert the problems that his repeated telephone calls have caused and that he should not do this again in future as this could constitute harassment.

commission for introducing new clients

We have so far established that accountants are keen to attract new clients and will use a number of different techniques to achieve this aim. One of these techniques could be to offer commission to someone for introducing new clients to the accountant or practice. In section 5.12.5 of the Guidelines it states that a member should not reward a third party for introducing a new client unless the client is fully aware of this arrangement and the third party is a member of a professional body that complies with a strict ethical code comparable with the AAT Guidelines on professional ethics.

Given these requirements, it is unlikely that an accountant would have to pay a commission to a third party for introducing new clients. However, it is acceptable for an accounting practice to offer a commission to employees for introducing new clients to the practice.

The exception to this is where an employee moves from one practice to another and tries to bring his/her clients to the new practice. This is not considered professional behaviour and will create bad will between the two accounting practices. This is not generally considered to be ethical behaviour on the part of the accountant and should be avoided.

In the following example we will demonstrate how this could happen in practice.

> ### example
>
> #### paying commission for introducing new clients
>
> Dominique Chapelle is a manager at Brown & Phips, a medium-sized accounting practice. She is keen to attract new clients and is trying to think of ways in which the firm can do this. So far she has come up with the following suggestions:
>
> - offering a commission to all employees for any new clients introduced to the practice
> - offering existing clients a discount on their fees for introducing new clients to the practice
> - asking the practice's bank if they would be willing to introduce new clients to the practice in return for an introductory fee
>
> Which of these suggestions is ethically acceptable?
>
> There is no reason why Brown & Phips should not offer commission to its employees for introducing new clients to the practice, provided they are not clients of a practice for which the employee has recently worked.
>
> When offering an existing client or the bank an incentive to introduce new clients, Brown & Phips must be very careful to ensure that the prospective client is aware of this arrangement and that the existing client or the bank are governed by appropriate ethical standards.

It is worth noting that most banks would not accept payment for introducing new clients to accounting practices, as this could be seen by third parties to compromise their independence.

PRACTICE NAMES AND LETTERHEADS

practice names

Most accountancy firms are named after past and/or present partners in the practice. For example the firm Osborne and Lynn will either currently have partners called Osborne and/or Lynn or will have had founding members with these names. A name that is derived in this way will usually be acceptable under the Guidelines.

Some accountants, however, will choose to style their practices in a different way.

Section 5.13.1 of the Guidelines states:

'A practice name should be consistent with the dignity of the profession in the sense that it should not project an image inconsistent with that of a professional practice bound to high ethical and technical standards.'

The key words here are 'consistent with the dignity of the profession'.

What this means is that when a practice is deciding what to call itself it should be careful that the name it chooses is not frivolous (silly), misleading, offensive or rude. The name should be sensible and appropriate for a profession that prides itself on its high ethical and technical standards.

For example an accounting practice should not be called 'Sam's Tax Evaders', 'Super Cheap Accountants' or 'Men Only Accountants!'. In the case of 'Sam's Tax Evaders' this name could be misleading as it infers that the firm will help its clients to evade paying tax, which is illegal. The name 'Super Cheap Accountants' suggests that the practice will be charging very low fees for its services which are therefore likely to fall short of the high standards expected of the accounting profession. 'Men Only Accountants' could be seen as offensive as it suggests that the practice discriminates against women.

Two specific ways in which a practice name could be misleading are described in Section 5.13.3 of the Guidelines. These are:

(i) **'a practice with a limited number of offices should not describe itself as 'international' merely on the grounds that one of them is overseas;**

(ii) **It would be misleading if there was a real risk that the practice name could be confused with the name of another practice, even if the member(s) of the practice could lay justifiable claim to the name'**

There now follows an example of a situation where the name of a practice could be misleading.

---

example

what's in a name?

Toby Andrews and Michelle White are both members of the AAT and have decided to set up a practice together. They have decided that they will call the practice Andrews & White and are just about to register the name and get stationery printed. Toby is reading the local paper and sees an advertisement for Andrew White Accountants, a firm based in a town about 20 miles away.

Should Toby and Michelle go ahead and name their practice Andrews & White?

Toby and Michelle can, quite justifiably, lay claim to the name Andrews & White as it is simply both their surnames combined and follows the traditional custom of naming a practice after the principals. However, it would be easy for this to be confused with the other practice named Andrew White Accountants which could mislead clients as to which firm they were employing.

Toby and Michelle then hit upon the idea of naming their practice White & Andrews Accountants, which would then get over the potential confusion over names.

The Guidelines also state in Section 5.13.2 that:

'A practice name must comply with partnership and company law as appropriate, and, in the UK, with the Business Names Act 1985.'

As part of your studies you are not expected to know this legislation in detail, but you should know that there are legal rules that restrict the name that an accountant chooses for his/her practice.

letterheads

Most organisations will have headed paper which they use for all their written communications. Accountants are no exception to this and will display their name and logos on all letterheads, documents and other stationery.

Letterheads should be of an acceptable professional standard, ie they should be clear, in good taste and consistent with the dignity of the profession. It is acceptable for the letterhead to include words such as Tax Advisers and Management Consultants provided the member(s) can show that they have expertise in that particular area.

A typical suitable letterhead is shown below.

TR

Thomson & Rice
Chartered Certified Accountants
24 Abbey Chambers, Woolchester, WO7 6GF
Tel 01909 627323 Fax 01909 627333

ACCOUNTING SERVICES, TAXATION ADVISERS, MANAGEMENT CONSULTANTS

Chapter Summary

- A letter of engagement is sent to a client whenever an accountant is employed to act for a client.

- The letter of engagement should give details of the nature of the assignment, the timetable and the way in which the fees will be calculated. It should also show the respective responsibilities of the accountant and the client.

- Accountants are entitled to be paid for the work that they carry out.

- The fees that an accountant charges should be based on the skills and knowledge and the level of training and experience needed for the assignment, the time that the assignment will take and the level of responsibility that the work entails.

- Accountants fees are normally based on an agreed rate per hour or day for different levels of staff involved in the work.

- An accountant can quote a fee that is lower than the client is currently paying provided that this does not affect the quality of the work and he/she does not intend to increase the fee once the work has been started.

- Fees can be charged on a contingent or a percentage basis provided they are not for a financial reporting assignment and do not create a self-interest threat to the accountant's independence.

- When clients choose to change their accountants it may be because they are unhappy with the service they are getting, or because they believe they can get a cheaper or better service elsewhere.

- When a client changes accountant the new accountant should check to ensure that the client has told the existing accountant of the change and has given them permission to co-operate with the new accountant.

- New accountants should request professional clearance from existing accountants before they accept an assignment for a new client.

- A statement made about a client in a professional clearance letter will not be viewed as malicious or defamatory provided the accountant honestly believes it to be true.

- When promoting their services, accountants should ensure that the advertisements are consistent with the dignity of the accounting profession.

- When an accounting practice is advertising its services it must comply with legal and regulatory requirements relating to advertising.

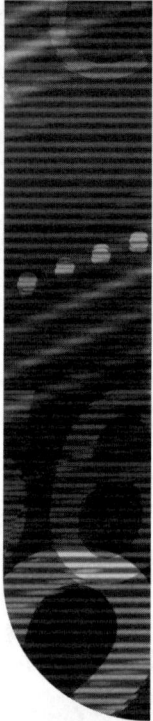

- When referring to fees in advertising material an accountant must take care not to mislead potential clients as to the services to be provided or the basis of current and future fees.

- Comparisons made in advertising with other accounting practices must be objective; relate to the same service; be factual and verifiable; and not discredit or denigrate the other practice.

- Members must not promote themselves in a way that could be seen as harassment of potential clients.

- Accountants will often pay commission to their employees for introducing new clients to the practice provided the employee is not 'poaching' these clients from a practice that he/she has previously worked for.

- The custom is that most accounting practices are named after past and/or present partners in the practice.

- When an accounting practice is deciding what to call itself it should choose a name that is consistent with the dignity of the accounting profession.

- Accountants' letterheads must be of an acceptable professional standard and should be clear and in good taste.

Key Terms		
letter of engagement	written confirmation of the work to be undertaken by the accountant and the extent of his/her responsibilities and those of the client	
professional clearance	a request for professional clearance is made by the new accountant to the existing accountant to ensure that there are no issues about the client that the new accountant should know about	
contingent fees	fees that will only be paid if a specified result is obtained	
defamation	to damage someone's reputation by saying or writing bad things about them which are not true	
qualified privilege	an accountant should not have to pay damages to a client for defamatory statements provided the accountant made these statements without malice	
denigrate	to say that another firm is not good at what they do	
harassment	annoying or upsetting a client by repeatedly contacting them	

answers to the asterisked (*) questions are to be found at the back of this book.

Student Activities

6.1* (a) What is the purpose of a letter of engagement?

(b) State five points that should be included in a letter of engagement.

6.2* A partner in the firm of accountants that you work for is due to attend a meeting with a new client tomorrow and has asked you to calculate the fees that the practice should charge this client. The partner has provided you with the following estimates of the time the assignment will take.

- two Trainees for four days each

- one Senior for three days

- one Manager for a day and a half day

- four hours of a Partner's time

Your firm's charge-out rates are as follows:

Trainee   £190   per day

Senior   £320   per day

Manager   £450   per day

Partner   £150   per hour

Using this information calculate how much the estimate for fees should be.

6.3* You work for Savadge & Oxley, a medium-sized accounting practice. On Monday morning you receive two telephone calls that each relate to fees. Details of each of the calls are as follows:

Call 1

An existing client asks you if you would be prepared to carry out some debt recovery work for him as he is currently having real difficulty obtaining payment from two of his largest customers. He suspects that they may be in financial difficulty. The client says that he would like your fee to be a percentage of the amount that you manage to recover from these customers.

Call 2

A potential client with whom you had an introductory meeting last week calls to discuss fees. She takes a hard line and tells you that Savadge & Oxley will have to save them £4,000 on their current fees charged by their existing accountants in order to get the work.

(a)   Give reasons why Savadge & Oxley should/should not accept the debt recovery work for the existing client on this basis.

(b)   What points should Savadge & Oxley consider when deciding what fees they should quote for the potential new client?

6.4*   You work for Savadge & Oxley, a medium-sized accounting practice (see Activity 6.3). Later in the day you receive a telephone call from another potential client who says that he would now like to go ahead and change to your firm. You explain to him that you will need authority from him to contact his existing accountants to obtain professional clearance. The line goes quiet and then he says that he is not prepared to give that authority and if you give him a list of what you need he will get it for you.

What should you do in this situation? Give reasons for your decision.

6.5   Savadge & Oxley are about to embark on a new marketing campaign in the hope that they will substantially increase the number of clients and consequently the fees earned by the practice.

The following suggestions have been made by the employees of Savadge & Oxley as possible things to include in the advertising:

(a)   'Say how much cheaper we are than other firms.'

(b)   'Offer a free introductory consultation for all new clients.'

(c)   'Offer a 20% discount in the first year for all new clients.'

(d)   'Say that we are the biggest and the best in town!'

(e)   'Give employees a commission for introducing new clients.'

(f)   'Pay a bonus to new employees who join Savadge & Oxley if they bring some of their clients with them!'

(g)   'Call all the local businesses we can think of and suggest that they change accountants and use us instead.'

For each of these suggestions decide whether they can ethically be used to advertise the services of Savadge & Oxley. Give reasons for your answers.

6.6 Sally Williams and Geoffrey Blythe are both members of the AAT and are about to set up in practice together. When they are deciding on a name for the practice Geoff jokingly suggests they should be called 'Sal & Geoff's Great Big Accounting Firm!'

Sally suggests that they should take the customary route and call the firm Williams & Blythe. Later in the day Geoffrey decides to look in the Phone Directory to see what names other accounting practices have chosen and realises that there is a small local firm called William Blythe Accountants.

Explain, giving reasons, why each of these names would be or would not be acceptable for their accounting practice.

This chapter considers some of the legal issues that an accountant in public practice may face when carrying out assignments for clients. It also covers the legal issues relating to money laundering which affect accountants in public practice and those who are employed in industry.

This chapter covers:

■ *the legal position relating to the ownership of a client's books and records*

■ *situations where an accountant can legitimately hold on to a client's documents until the client pays his/her fees*

■ *how long an accountant must hold on to books, working papers and other documents before they can legally dispose of them*

■ *situations where an accountant may be open to legal action and to pay damages to a client for failing to act with the necessary due care*

■ *the responsibilities of accountants in relation to money laundering*

PERFORMANCE CRITERIA COVERED

unit 32: PROFESSIONAL ETHICS

Element 32.3

develop, maintain and apply ethics in public practice

F   *Identify scope of professional liability.*

H   *Give advice to clients on retention of books, working papers and other documents.*

OWNERSHIP OF BOOKS AND RECORDS

what are books and records?

Anyone who works in an office will know that a huge amount of information is generated on a daily basis. This can be in various forms, for example paper documents, computer files, CDs and emails. When we refer to 'books and records' we are not simply talking about the paper documents, we include all of the above in this category.

legal considerations

In our normal everyday lives we would expect that if we create a document then it belongs to us or to the business for which we work. For example, if we write a report at work it is the property of the organisation for which we work.

There may, however, be circumstances where the decision as to who owns a document is not so clear-cut. For example, if you were to write a letter and send it to someone, does the letter belong to you or the person that you have sent it to? Or in the example of the report that you have written, if you are writing that report specifically for a client of your firm, does the report belong to you or to the client? These questions are less easy to answer.

When there is a legal relationship between a client and a professional person, such as an accountant, the rules on ownership of books and records are based on a combination of statute and case law.

Statute law is the law of the land, created by Parliament, whereas **case law** is law that has been established based on previous legal decisions in courts of law.

When a member enters into a contract with a client he/she must be fully aware of the legal principles that govern the contract. The member should also make sure that the respective rights and responsibilities of the member and the client are covered in the letter of engagement that they issue at the beginning of the assignment.

to whom do books and records belong?

Section 6.1.2 of the Guidelines states that as well as the requirements of the law, when deciding whether documents and records belong to the member or the client the following points need to be considered:

- the type of contract (a legally binding agreement) between the member and the client (this is normally set out in the letter of engagement)
- the capacity in which the member acts for the client, ie whether the accountant is acting as an agent or not
- the purpose for which the documents exist or are created

Note that in law an agent is someone who acts for someone else, for example an estate 'agent' who sets up a house sale for a client (who is known as the 'principal').

The general rule relating to the accounting profession is that where a member acts as a principal – ie getting on with his/her own job – all documents that he/she creates during an assignment, such as notes and working papers, belong to the member.

The exception to this is the documents that the client specifically asks the member to create on their behalf, eg financial statements, which will belong to the client.

The two main types of work that a member performs for a client are accounting and taxation. We will now look at each of these and decide in each case who owns the documents and records.

accountancy work

If a member is preparing a client's financial statements, the working papers that the member produces during the assignment belong to the member and the financial statements that he/she creates belong to the client. If, however, the assignment is to create the accounting records for the client by entering the transactions in the client's ledgers then these accounting records also belong to the client. It all depends on what the client as 'principal' asks the accountant as 'agent' to do.

taxation work

When a member is carrying out taxation work for a client, such as preparing and submitting formal tax returns to HMRC, he/she is acting as the client's agent and therefore the documents completed will normally belong to the client.

If the member is providing tax advice to a client on request, then any written documents that he/she produces for the client will belong to the client. Any incidental working papers that the member produces will belong to the member.

correspondence

At the beginning of this chapter we questioned whether a letter that you send belongs to you or to the person who receives it. We will now look at the same situation where the correspondence is between a member and his/her client.

Section 6.1.8 of the Guidelines states:

'Letters received by the member from the client, copies of letters from the member to the client and notes made by the member of discussions with the client belong, under UK law, to the member.'

We can see from this that in most cases correspondence between a member and the client belongs to the member.

If, however, a third party becomes involved then ownership of the documents depends on the question of whether the member is acting as an agent ('person in the middle') for the client or not.

If a member is acting as an agent for the client, letters that the member receives from a third party and letters sent to the third party belong to the client. A good example of this is where a member is carrying out tax work for a client. In this case the member will normally be acting as an agent for the client and will be sending and receiving letters to and from HM Revenue & Customs. All letters that the member receives from the tax authorities belong to the client as the member is acting on the client's behalf. All copies of letters sent by the member to the tax authorities also belong to the client for the same reason.

This may all seem confusing, but can be summarised as follows:

- if the client has asked for a document to be produced as part of an assignment then this document will belong to the client
- if the member is acting as an agent on behalf of the client then the documents will belong to the client
- in all other cases the documents will belong to the member

The example that follows illustrates the question of who owns documents and records in different circumstances.

example

a question of ownership

Zahid Anwar is an accountant in public practice. For several years he has been working for a client, Maximus Ltd, preparing tax returns and producing the company's financial statements. He has just completed the financial statements for the current year and is having a final meeting with the Finance Director and the Finance Supervisor. Having presented them with the final version of the financial statements Zahid asks if there are any further questions.

> The Finance Supervisor asks: 'When you did the tax return earlier in the year you gave us lots of documents, working papers and copies of letters. Why don't you give us all the working papers you produced when you were preparing the financial statements?'
>
> What should Zahid tell her?
>
> Zahid should explain that when he is preparing tax schedules and completing tax returns for Maximus Ltd, he is acting as the client's agent. In this situation all the documents and records that are produced belong to Maximus Ltd. When he is preparing the financial statements for the client these financial statements belong to Maximus Ltd, but Zahid's working papers belong to Zahid.

LIEN

A lien can be defined as: **'the right to retain possession of another's property until an obligation is paid'**. This means that a person can hold on to something that belongs to one of his/her debtors until the debt is paid. There are two types of lien, a **general lien** that gives the creditor the right to hold on to **any** of the debtor's goods, and a **particular lien** that relates only to goods that form part of a specific transaction between the two parties.

So why are liens relevant to accountants in public practice? When a member has carried out work on documents that belong to a client and the client has not paid the member, under UK law the member has a 'particular lien' over these documents. This means that the member is allowed to hold on to these documents and records until his/her fees are paid. For example a member may be working for a client preparing a draft income tax return for a client. If the client then refuses to pay the member's fees for this work he/she can hold on to the draft return until the fees are paid.

Section 6.2.2 of the Guidelines details certain conditions that must exist in order for a member to have a right of lien. These can be summarised as follows:

- the documents that the member is holding on to must belong to the client and not to a third party

- the member must have obtained the documents by proper means

- the member must actually have carried out work on the documents and must have provided the client with a detailed fee note, and the fees must still remain outstanding for this work (ie not for past work)

> **example**
>
> **a lien over documents and records**
>
> Holly Astley is a partner at Chance & Astley Accountants. One of the practice's clients, Collingwood Limited is refusing to pay the fee for tax work that Chance & Astley have carried out. The client says that the fees are higher than they were initially quoted. Holly has provided Collingwood Limited with a copy of the quote that clearly states the fees to be charged.
>
> Chance and Astley have also prepared the personal income tax return for the Gerald Collingwood, the client's Managing Director, and have been paid for this work.
>
> In these circumstances can Holly retain the tax documents relating to either Collingwood Limited or Gerald Collingwood until the fees are paid?
>
> Chance & Astley have a particular lien over the tax documents that relate to Collingwood Limited because the practice has carried out work on them and has provided the client with a fee note for the work. Therefore Holly can quite legitimately hold on to these documents until the fee is paid.
>
> Whilst it may be tempting for Holly to hold on to the documents that relate to the work done for Gerald Collingwood, Chance & Astley do not have a lien over these documents as the fees for this work have been paid and the documents belong to a third party. Therefore, Holly cannot retain the personal tax documents that belong to Gerald Collingwood.

There are some special rules that relate to the statutory books and accounting records of companies, and also where documents are claimed by an Administrator or Liquidator of a company. Further guidance on these matters can be obtained from the AAT or from a solicitor, but you do not need to know about these for your studies.

RETENTION OF DOCUMENTS AND RECORDS

why retain documents and records?

There is a general principle that once a certain amount of time has passed since an event has occurred, a legal action cannot be brought in relation to that event.

It is always possible that a client who is unhappy with work that has been carried out by his/her accountant may decide to bring some kind of legal action against the accountant. It is, therefore, important that the accountant holds on to all relevant documentation until enough time has passed that the client is no longer legally entitled to being proceedings against him/her.

how long should documents be retained?

There are a number of laws in the UK that specify the periods of time within which legal action must be taken. If, however, there is no particular statute (law) that specifies time limits, the **Limitation Act 1980** sets out the default position.

The time limit for legal actions brought under simple contract law is six years. This means that a dissatisfied client could bring legal proceedings against his/her accountant any time up until the end of the six year period. It is therefore, recommended that accountants in public practice actually retain books, working papers and other documents for seven years (ie an additional year to the six years) to allow a safety margin. The AAT Guidelines (Section 6.3.4) state that taxation records should be retained for eight years.

If a member is in any doubt about the length of time that documents and records should be retained it is important that they take legal advice from a solicitor.

PROFESSIONAL LIABILITY OF MEMBERS

a definition of liability

Liability means **'having legal responsibility for something with the possibility of having to pay damages'**.

Liability can arise from a number of causes, including criminal acts, breach of contract and negligent acts.

In law **negligence** is a breach of a duty of care that is implied in a particular situation or relationship. For example, a railway company has a duty of care for the safe transit of its passengers and an accountant has a duty of care to carry out assignments in a skilled and professional manner. If the railway company fails to observe safety measures (such as red signals) and the accountant makes mistakes in a tax return, they are both held to be negligent. The AAT Guidelines on Professional Ethics deal with liability for professional negligence on the part of a member. In the case of members of the AAT, **professional negligence** may occur if a client, to whom the member owes a duty of care, suffers a financial loss that can be proved is the fault of the member. An example of this is given on page 120.

minimising the risk of professional negligence

For all assignments the following points should be covered to ensure that the possibility of a client suing a member for professional negligence is minimised:

- A member should ensure that before taking on an assignment the exact duties to be included (and equally as important, excluded) in the assignment are written down and agreed by both the member and the client. This would normally be done in the letter of engagement.

- If further duties are added to an assignment then the member should ensure that these are also written down and agreed by both parties.

- Where a member gives a client advice without having been provided with all the information he/she needs, the member must make sure that the client is aware of any limitations to this advice.

- If the member prepares unaudited accounts or financial statements for a client he/she must clearly mark on the documents that they are confidential and solely for the private use of the client.

- If a member is asked for a reference by a third party, (eg from a property company regarding the client's ability to pay rent) the member should state that this is an opinion and given without financial responsibility on the part of the member.

- If an assignment is very complex a member should take specialist advice or suggest that the client does so.

disclaimer of professional liability

When a member produces documents for a client, financial statements, for example, he/she may decide to attach a statement disclaiming professional liability. The exact wording of such a disclaimer will vary depending on the type of documents involved. The following is a good example:

'No responsibility for loss to any person acting or refraining from acting as a result of any material in this document can be accepted by X (insert the member's name or practice name). Professional advice should be taken before applying the contents of this document to your particular circumstances.'

It would seem that including a statement such as this is a simple and easy way for a member to cover him/herself and stop any possibility of legal action. However such a clause cannot be relied on in all circumstances and it is possible that a disclaimer may be seen by a court of law as an attempt by an accountant to escape his/her legal responsibility and therefore disregarded.

professional indemnity insurance

All members hope that they will never be put in the position where a client brings a legal case against them for professional negligence. However, it is possible that at some time this may happen. Section 6.4.8 of the AAT Guidelines says that all members in practice should ensure that they have adequate **professional indemnity insurance**. This type of insurance is taken out by an accountant (or other professional) as cover against legal liability to compensate a third party (normally a client) who has sustained injury, loss or damage through a breach in the accountant's duty of care.

We will now look at an example where the issue of professional liability could arise.

---

example

a question of professional liability

Christopher Matthews works as an accountant in practice. He has recently received a request from the Managing Director of one of his clients to provide him with some personal advice on inheritance tax. Christopher has no experience in this area of taxation and has never given advice on inheritance tax before.

Christopher is considering reading up on this area of tax and taking on this assignment. However, he thinks it would be a good idea to make sure his professional indemnity insurance is up-to-date and to put a disclaimer of professional liability in the letter of engagement and in any documentation that he produces for the client.

Is this appropriate professional and ethical behaviour on Christopher's part?

If Christopher is unsure of his expertise regarding inheritance tax he should ensure that he gets the necessary advice and guidance from an appropriately qualified person. He should only take on the assignment if he considers that he has the professional and technical competence to carry out the work satisfactorily.

It would be unprofessional for Christopher to rely on a disclaimer of professional liability to cover the risk that he may not carry out the work properly. It is also unlikely that a court would allow him to rely on this should the client bring a legal action for damages against him were his advice to result in the client losing money.

All accountants should have professional indemnity insurance. But this should not be used as a 'safety net' in situations where an accountant does not have the necessary skills to carry out an assignment.

MONEY LAUNDERING

a definition of money laundering

In Chapter 3 we looked at the disclosure of confidential information where there has been an infringement of the law. The example we used for this was money laundering which was defined as:

'to move illegally acquired cash through financial systems so that it appears to be legally acquired.'

Put simply, this means using money gained illegally – eg through terrorist funding, drug dealing or other criminal activities – so that the money is 'laundered' or 'washed' and then appears to be 'clean' and legally obtained. We will now look at the issue of money laundering in greater detail.

responsibilities for reporting money laundering

The combined effect of the **Proceeds of Crime Act 2002 (POCA)**, the **Serious Organised Crime and Police Act 2005**, and the **Money Laundering Regulations 2003** means that where an accountant or practice has knowledge, suspicion, or reasonable grounds for suspicion that a client or an employer is involved with illegally obtained money there is a legal requirement to report this to the National Criminal Intelligence Service (NCIS). Note also that if the member is working in an organisation which has appointed a Money Laundering Reporting Officer, the matter should be reported to that Officer.

Practices and employers must also have training and internal procedures in place to ensure that they comply with the reporting requirements above. If these procedures are not in place the accountant may be liable for a fine or imprisonment or both.

Clearly this an important legal issue that the accounting profession takes very seriously. Members and student members must ensure that they are familiar with their employer's internal procedures for reporting suspicions of money laundering. Employers must ensure that all their staff have been provided with adequate training on their legal obligations in respect of money laundering and the firms anti-money laundering procedures.

tipping off

The Proceeds of Crime Act has created an offence of 'tipping off'. This is where someone who knows, or thinks they know that, a report of money laundering has been made to the NCIS warns (or 'tips off') the person(s) suspected. Where this happens the person who 'tips off' the suspect is liable to be prosecuted as well as the person who is carrying out the money laundering.

An accountant who discovers that an employer or a client is potentially money laundering must report his/her suspicions to the NCIS. They must ensure, however, that they do not make the employer or client aware of this as this would be considered tipping off.

Although tipping off is an offence, an accountant is entitled to advise his/her clients in general terms about the issue of money laundering.

The following example illustrates the serious implications of money laundering.

example

a case of money laundering

Wilfred Joyce is an accountant in public practice. One of his clients is an antiques dealer called Louis Kans. One Friday Wilfred receives a telephone enquiry from Louis, who says that a customer is in the shop asking to buy a piece of furniture for £11,000. The customer is offering to pay Louis in cash.

What should Wilfred advise in this situation?

Louis has been offered a large amount of cash but does not really know where it has come from. Although the customer may have good reasons for having such a large amount of cash there is a risk that it may not have been gained through legal means.

As Wilfred's objective in this situation is to ensure that his client does not breach the Money Laundering Regulations 2003, he should advise Louis to identify the customer and verify the source of the cash before accepting it, thus satisfying himself that the cash is not the proceeds of some crime.

If despite Wilfred's advice Louis then goes on and deals with the customer on a cash basis then Wilfred will have no option but to report him to the NCIS.

accepting new clients

In Chapter 6 we described the methods accountants use to obtain new clients. There may, however, be occasions where an accountant is not able to take on a new client. This could be because the accountant does not have sufficient staff with the appropriate expertise to carry out the work for the client. Or it could simply be that the accountant does not feel that it is appropriate to take on the client. One of the reasons for this could relate to money laundering.

The Money Laundering Regulations 2003 require that as soon as it is reasonably practicable, accountants should obtain satisfactory evidence of the identity of a new client. The most common way of doing this is for the accountant to ask to see the client's passport or driving licence and a current utility bill showing the client's name and address.

Where the client is a business rather than an individual the accountant will not need to obtain evidence of the identity of all individuals involved in the business. Normally only the principal contacts and the people who control the business should be identified.

Chapter Summary

- The rules on ownership of books and records are mainly based on a combination of statute law and case law.

- If a client asks for a document to be produced as part of an assignment then this document will belong to the client.

- If an accountant is acting as an agent on behalf of a client (for example when performing tax work) then the documents will belong to the client.

- If a client fails to pay an accountant for work that he/she has performed, the accountant has a particular lien over the client's books and records and can hold on to them until the fees are paid.

- There are a number of laws in the UK that specify the length of time within which legal action must be taken.

- Accountants should ideally retain books, working paper and other documents for seven years before disposing of them (the law implies a requirement of a period of six years).

- Taxation records should be kept for eight years.

- Accountants have a professional duty of care when carrying out work for clients and have professional liability for the work that they carry out.

- Where a client suffers a loss as a result of work carried out by an accountant they may bring a legal action against the accountant for professional negligence.

- Accountants will sometimes include a disclaimer of professional liability in documents that they produce for clients in an attempt to minimise the risk of a case of professional negligence being brought against them.

- Members of the AAT should have sufficient professional indemnity insurance to cover against legal liability to compensate a client who has sustained loss through a breach of the accountant's duty of care.

- If a member has knowledge or a suspicion that a client or an employer is money laundering they must report this to the National Criminal Intelligence Service (NCIS).

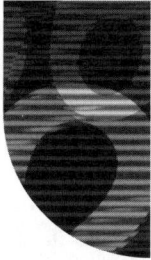

- Accountants must have training and internal procedures in place to ensure that they comply with the legal requirements and regulations relating to money laundering.

- It is an illegal offence to tip-off somebody who has been reported to the NCIS on suspicion of money laundering.

- Before accepting a new client an accountant must obtain documentary evidence to confirm the name and the identity of a new client.

Key Terms		
statute law	laws that are passed as acts of parliament and relate to the legal governance of the land
case law	law that has been established based upon legal decisions made in previous cases
lien	the right of an accountant to retain a client's books and records until the accountant's fees are paid
Limitation Act 1980	a statute which sets out the time limits for taking legal action
professional liability	the legal responsibility that a professional person has for work that they carry out that a client then relies on
professional negligence	this may occur where a client, to whom the member owes a duty of care, suffers a financial loss which can be proved is the fault of the accountant
disclaimer of professional liability	a clause that an accountant includes in a document in an attempt to minimise his/her liability relating to the information provided
professional indemnity insurance	insurance that an accountant takes out to cover any damages he/she may have to pay a client due to professional negligence
money laundering	moving illegally acquired cash through financial systems so that it appears to be legally acquired
Proceeds of Crime Act 2002	a statute that sets out the law in relation to financial gains made from illegal acts
Money Laundering Regulations 2003	the regulations governing the crime of money laundering
NCIS	National Criminal Intelligence Service
tipping off	warning an individual suspected of money laundering that he/she has been reported to the NCIS

Student Activities

answers to the asterisked (*) questions are to be found at the back of this book.

7.1*   Explain who would normally 'own' each of the following documents?

    (a)   An accountant's working papers when he/she is preparing a client's financial statements.

    (b)   Correspondence between an accountant and Her Majesty's Revenue & Customs where the accountant is preparing the client's tax return.

    (c)   A report on costing that a client has specifically asked her accountant to produce.

7.2*   You are a manager at McBrides Accountants. One of the practice's clients, a hairdressing salon called Heavenly Hair is refusing to pay the fee for the work that McBrides have carried out for them. The owner Jason Blue says he is unhappy with the service that he received from McBrides and is not prepared to pay the full amount charged in the fee note.

McBrides also prepare tax returns for Natural Nails, a beauty parlour owned by Jennifer Blue, Jason's wife. Natural Nails is located in the same premises as Heavenly Hair. Jennifer Blue has paid McBrides latest invoice for this work.

In these circumstances are you justified in retaining the tax documents relating to either Heavenly Hair or Natural Nails until Heavenly Hair's fees are paid? Give reasons for your answer.

7.3*   Melissa Strauss, a practising accountant, has been approached by Allan Salt, one of her existing clients, to provide some detailed advice on the tax implications of a business merger that he is considering. Although Melissa has some significant tax experience she is not clear as to exactly what level of expertise the client is expecting from her.

Explain how Melissa can protect herself from the risk of professional negligence in this situation.

7.4   Henry Tremlett works for a medium-sized accounting practice. One of his clients is a local second-hand car dealership which he regularly visits to complete their accounting records.

During a recent visit the owner of the car dealership has agreed to sell a car to a customer for £11,000. The customer appears anxious to complete the purchase and offers to pay for the car in cash. What should Henry advise in this situation, and why?

7.5   Before taking on a potential new client what sort of information should an accountant obtain from the client, and why?

Answers to student activities

CHAPTER 1 – PRINCIPLES OF PROFESSIONAL ETHICS

1.1 There are two main points that arise from this situation.

- The fact that the solicitor is disclosing confidential information about a number of his clients to his dinner partner may or may not be appropriate as you have no way of knowing who this person is. The issue for the solicitor is that he is speaking loudly enough for you to hear his conversation which means that other diners in the restaurant will also be able to hear it.

  However, this is not your issue and whilst you may feel that he is acting in an unethical manner there is no obligation on your part to do anything about this.

- The fact that the solicitor is considering leaving the partnership is likely to have a significant impact on the solicitor's firm. However, this is confidential information and consequently you cannot disclose it to the other partners in the firm. You should make the solicitor aware that you overheard his conversation and that whilst you are aware that this is confidential you would encourage him to discuss his plans with the other partners.

1.2 The completion of expense claims by members of staff assumes both honesty and integrity on their part. There is sometimes a culture in organisations for people to feel justified in claiming more on their expenses than they are entitled to, however this amounts to fraud. It is important to ensure that staff within G Verdi & Co are aware of the need for honesty and integrity and consequently to promote strong ethical values within the firm.

Consequently, you should not sign the expense claim until you have investigated the two issues that you have identified. If after looking into these issues you still believe that the form is inaccurate you should arrange a meeting with the member of staff. At this meeting you should point out the errors in his claim and explain to him that it is unacceptable to claim more in expenses than you are entitled to. You should also explain that he must now amend his expense claim before you are prepared to approve it and make him aware that in future you will be reviewing his expense claims in detail.

1.3 There are several options that G Verdi & Co can take:

- They could decline the assignment on the basis that they do not have necessary skills to carry out the training.

- They could employ someone with the appropriate training skills to deliver the 'Credit Control without tears' training course. The problem with this option is that unless the new member of staff has good technical skills the staff of G Verdi & Co will have to 'train' the new membe of staff.

- They could arrange for relevant members of staff to attend an appropriate course to develop their training skills, thereby allowing them to deliver the 'Credit control without tears' course with confidence.

Whichever of the three options that G Verdi & Co decide upon they are ensuring that they do not take on an assignment which they are not competent to carry out.

CHAPTER 2 – OBJECTIVITY AND PROFESSIONAL ETHICS

2.1 (a) Taking a principle-based approach you would explain to the client that he should make HM Revenue and Customs (HMRC) aware immediately of the fact that he has failed to complete these tax returns and that he intends to pay the outstanding tax as soon as possible. Taking this approach you have identified the objective – which is that the client pays his outstanding tax as soon as possible – and you have given the client the necessary professional advice to allow him to do so.

(b) Taking a rule-based approach you would report him to the relevant authority straightaway for failing to complete a tax return for any of the previous four years.

Note: if the client does not take your advice under the principle-based approach you will be faced with no alternative but to report the client to the relevant authorities anyway.

2.2 In order for accountants to remain objective they must always be, and be seen to be, independent. The issue in this situation is that the family connection between Nisha and Henderson and Brighton's client may present a conflict of interest for Nisha which could threaten her independence and hence her objectivity.

The AAT Guidelines on Professional Ethics states (in Section 3.1.4) that an accountant must be 'seen to be independent' (independent in appearance). This means that the accountant must ensure that any third party can be confident that the accountant always behaves independently and has avoided doing anything that may question this independence.

Henderson and Brighton can quite legitimately decide not to employ Nisha on this basis – they may even have a policy where this type of situation prohibits a person from being employed by the firm.

If Henderson and Brighton believe that Nisha is the right person for the job as manager then they can offer her the job. However, they will have to ensure that she does not work on the accounts of her father's company and that she has no connection whatever with their preparation. If this is ensured then there will be no conflict of interest for Nisha and consequently the firm's independence and objectivity will not be compromised.

2.3 The offer from Far To Go is clearly a very generous one and it would be very tempting for Henderson and Brighton to accept it. However, the acceptance of gifts, services, favours or hospitality from a client can threaten the independence of an accountant.

In this case there is a risk that these gifts could influence the work performed and decisions made by Henderson and Brighton. There is no doubt that a 40% discount would result in a substantial cost saving for the staff of Henderson and Brighton. However, if a third party were to become aware of this arrangement they could quite legitimately consider that Henderson and Brighton might be influenced by the financial benefit that their staff are receiving from Far To Go.

You should therefore contact Far To Go and explain that whilst this is a very generous offer on their part, you will have to decline.

CHAPTER 3 – CONFIDENTIALITY AND TAXATION SERVICES

3.1   One of the fundamental principles of professional ethics is confidentiality. Members of the AAT have a duty of confidentiality not to disclose information obtained about a client or employer during the course of their professional work.

In this situation, by talking to Jane about Booth Ltd, Pierre has breached his duty of confidentiality to the client. Despite the fact that Jane and Pierre work for the same firm of accountants Pierre should not be discussing confidential client information in this way. There is also the risk that whilst discussing client matters in the public area of the offices, employees of the other four firms in the building could overhear confidential information.

Jane is also discussing confidential client information. However, in her case she no longer works for the client. This does not affect the duty of confidentiality that Jane has to Castle & Co. The AAT Guidelines on professional ethics say that a member's duty of confidentiality continues even after the end of the relationship between the member and the client or employer. Therefore the fact that Castle & Co is no longer one of Jane's clients makes no difference to her duty to keep information about the client confidential.

3.2   (a)   A member of the AAT is permitted to disclose confidential information about a client or employer in the following circumstances:

■   When the member has been authorised by the client to do so.

■   When there is a requirement by law to disclose confidential information. This may be as evidence in a court of law, or when the law has been broken and the information has to be disclosed to the relevant authorities.

■   When the member has a professional duty to disclose the information. This could be to comply with technical or ethical requirements, to protect the professional interests of the member in legal proceedings, or in response to an inquiry by the AAT or by a regulatory body.

(b)   If an accountant is in any doubt as to whether he/she should disclose confidential information, or where he/she is unclear as to how much he/she should disclose, he/she should consider taking appropriate legal advice or should contact the AAT Ethics Advice Line.

3.3   Financial information regarding your employer is confidential. Therefore, as an employee of Lambretti & Clarke you should not disclose any information about the company to the new suppliers unless you have been authorised to do so.

In these circumstances you should speak to your supervisor to find out who within Lambretti & Clarke has the necessary authority to decide whether this information can be disclosed. You should only provide the information requested by the supplier when you have authority, preferably in writing, from the appropriate person. You should also ensure that when you provide the information to the new supplier you make it clear that the information is provided only for the supplier to ascertain the credit worthiness of Lambretti & Clarke and for no other purpose.

CHAPTER 4 - ETHICS AND THE EMPLOYED ACCOUNTANT

4.1   Before taking any action in this situation you must be sure of your facts, as it is a serious step to accuse the accounts supervisor of defrauding the company. However, if this is a genuine concern, you should raise it with a more senior member of Flowmow staff such as the Financial Controller. It would not be appropriate to accuse the accounts supervisor directly because if your concerns are unfounded this could make your future working relationship difficult.

It will then become a matter for the Financial Controller to investigate, however, if he/she chooses not to take any action you would have to take it to a higher level of management within Flowmow. Only in the unlikely event that no action was taken by the organisation would you have to consider resigning as a consequence of this issue.

4.2   In this case there is clearly a difference of opinion between you and the payroll supervisor as to whether anything should be done about the employee who is fiddling his expenses. You should therefore raise the issue with a more senior member of staff, for example the payroll manager or financial controller. However, if all else fails the issue should be raised with one of Prestige's non-executive directors.

4.3   Clearly in this situation the directors are breaking the law by not declaring the sports cars as taxable benefits for the directors. This matter should be raised with your immediate superior and then if necessary higher up in the organisation. You should try hard to persuade the directors to disclose these cars and complete all the relevant documentation to notify the tax authorities that they are taxable benefits. If the directors of Splendid Ltd continue to act illegally you have no option but to resign, stating your reasons for resignation. It is possible that the threat of resignation may be sufficient to persuade the directors to comply with your request.

4.4 Dodgy Ltd are breaking the law in a number of different areas:

■ By failing to declare cash sales, they will produce inaccurate and deliberately misleading financial statements and will ultimately underpay on their corporation tax liability.

■ By allowing the directors to use cash for personal expenditure it is unlikely that this is being declared by the directors for income tax purposes.

■ By employing casual staff and not including them on the payroll they are acting illegally by breaking tax regulations.

■ By allowing casual staff to handle toxic substances without the necessary training or protective clothing they are breaking the legal requirements of Health & Safety regulations.

In this situation you could try to persuade the directors of Dodgy Ltd to stop acting illegally. However, it is probable that Dodgy is corrupt throughout the organisation, with staff at all levels involved in illegal activities.

You, therefore, have two available options.

Firstly, you could resign from the company, explaining the reasons for your resignation to the directors. The second option is to blow the whistle on Dodgy Ltd and report the illegal activities to the appropriate authorities. Given that the company is so deeply involved in illegal activities the second option of blowing the whistle would probably be the most appropriate. However it would be advisable to take legal advice before doing so.

CHAPTER 5 – INDEPENDENCE OF THE MEMBER IN PRACTICE

5.1 If Simon were to take on this new client this would work out to be nearly 25% of his firm's total annual fee income, including the new client. This would be a substantial proportion of Simon's total fee income and could represent a self-interest threat to Simon's firm's independence as the firm could become economically reliant on the new client. Therefore, in these circumstances, Simon should not accept the additional work that he is being offered.

In addition to the self-interest threat that this situation poses there is also an issue with regard to whether Simon's firm has the professional skills and expertise and the necessary resources to take on this new client. Simon's firm has no current experience of clients of a similar size and, in addition, may not have sufficient staff with the necessary expertise to carry out the assignment.

5.2 Section 5.2.7 of the Guidelines clearly states that where a member has been an employee of a potential client at any time in the previous two years this creates an insurmountable threat of self-review to the independence of that member. Therefore, you must immediately inform Jeff of your previous employment and suggest that George Broom & Son decline the assignment unless they have sufficient staff to ensure that you do not have to be involved in any way in this assignment.

5.3 Although Maurice and Anne-Marie are not husband and wife, there is a close relationship between them which is made even closer by the fact that they have now set up home together. This relationship constitutes a familiarity threat to Maurice's independence; consequently he should not agree to Anne-Marie's request and should instead recommend an alternative accountant to her.

5.4 There is no reason why Maddie should not attend the meeting with the potential investor. However, she must ensure that she remains totally objective throughout.

She must not take a strongly proactive stance on the client's behalf as this could be construed as going beyond her advisory role for Connor & Jackson and would have a serious negative effect on Maddie's independence.

Therefore, Maddie can agree to attend the meeting with the potential investor, and can, with Connor & Jackson's permission, discuss the financial statements of her client However, she should not give her opinion on the suitability of Conner & Jackson as an investment opportunity.

CHAPTER 6 – TAKING ON NEW CLIENTS

6.1 (a) A letter of engagement provides written confirmation of the work to be undertaken by the accountant and also the respective responsibilities of the accountant and the client. It should be agreed and signed by the accountant and the client.

(b) A letter of engagement should include:

- the nature of the assignment, ie whether it is accounting, taxation, audit or some other type of service

- details of any reports that are to be produced as part of the assignment

- the timetable for the assignment, including when the work is due to start and how long it is expected to take

- the responsibilities of the client, including the books and records that he/she is expected to produce

- the client's responsibility to detect errors and fraud

- details of how the accountant's fees are to be calculated and action that will be taken for unpaid fees

- ownership of books and records created during the assignment

- whether the accountant's work will be used by a third party

The answer should include any five of the above points.

6.2 The fees calculation should be made by applying the standard charge-out rates to the number of hours/days that the assignment will take at each level.

2 Trainees for 4 days at £190/day	=	2 x 4 x £190	=	£1,520
1 Senior for 3 days at £320/day	=	3 x £320	=	£960
1 Manager for 1.5 days at £450/day	=	1.5 x £450	=	£675
1 Partner for 4 hours at £150/hour	=	4 x £150	=	£600
Total fees estimate should be				£3,755

6.3   Call 1 – new client

Accountants will sometimes be asked to carry out work on a percentage basis because the client will not be able to pay the accountant's fees unless the assignment achieves the required result. In this case it seems likely that the client needs the money from his slow-paying customers in order to pay Savadge & Oxley for the debt recovery work. Alternatively a percentage fee could be used as an incentive for the accountant to achieve the best possible result.

There is no ethical reason why Savadge & Oxley should not accept the assignment on this basis and the only consideration will be whether the percentage that the client is offering is high enough to make the assignment worthwhile.

Call 2 – existing client

First, there is no reason why an accountant should not quote a lower fee than has been charged in a previous period provided it does not affect the quality of the work.

You will need to estimate what the fees should be for this potential client, based on Savadge & Oxley's standard charge-out rates, and the number of hours you expect the assignment to take. If this is lower than their existing fees by £4,000, or more, then you will be able to fulfil the requirement of the client for a £4,000 reduction in fees.

If the estimate is less than £4,000 lower than the potential client's existing fees then you have two choices, either:

- Quote £4,000 less than the client's existing fees and accept that the firm will make a reduced profit on the assignment.

- Quote for the assignment based on your estimate, explaining that the work cannot be carried out to the required standard for a fee lower than this.

6.4   As part of the change in accountants for this client Savadge & Oxley need to obtain professional clearance from the existing accountants. The client's refusal to give you authority to contact them means that this clearance cannot be obtained. Unless you can persuade the potential client to give you permission to contact them, and for them to co-operate freely with Savadge & Oxley, then you should decline the assignment.

CHAPTER 7 – LEGAL CONSIDERATIONS

7.1   (a)   If an accountant is preparing a client's financial statements the working papers that he/she produces during the assignment belong to the accountant and the financial statements that he/she creates belong to the client.

       (b)   Where an accountant is carrying out tax work for a client he/she will normally be acting as the client's agent. In this case all the correspondence between an accountant and Her Majesty's Revenue & Customs belong to the client.

       (c)   If a client has specifically asked for a document to be produced as part of an assignment then this documents belongs to the client. Therefore in this case the report will belong to the client.

7.2   McBrides have a particular lien over the tax documents that relate to Heavenly Hair as the practice has carried out work on them and has provided the client with a fee note for the work. Therefore McBrides can quite legitimately hold on to these documents until the fee is paid.

Despite the fact that Jason and Jennifer are married, McBrides do not have a lien over Natural Nail's documents as the fees for this work have been paid and the documents belong to a third party. Therefore, the tax documents that belong to Natural Nails cannot be retained.

7.3   Melissa should ensure the following:

- the exact duties to be included and excluded in the assignment should be written down in a letter of engagement for the assignment and agreed by both Melissa and the client

- if further duties are added to an assignment then Melissa should ensure that these are also written down and agreed with the client

- if Melissa considers at any stage that the information that she is provided with is not sufficient she must make sure that the client is aware of any limitations this might have on the advice she gives

- she must clearly mark on any documents that she produces that they are confidential and solely for the private use of the client

- if the assignment is very complex Melissa should take specialist advice or suggest that the client does so

In addition to the above points Melissa should ensure that she always has sufficient professional indemnity insurance.

Unit 32
Professional Ethics

Simulation 1: Clarke Homer

Element coverage

32.1   Apply general principles and procedures for ethical compliance expected within the accounting sector.

32.2   Develop, maintain and apply ethics in employer/employee situations.

32.3   Develop, maintain and apply ethics in public practice.

Scenario and contents

This Simulation is based on Clarke Homer, a firm of accountants. The tasks include:

- assessing ethical issues relating to staff behaviour
- advertising for and obtaining new clients
- procedures relating to confidential information
- ensuring professional and technical competence
- obtaining continuing professional development
- procedures for holding client monies
- appropriate bases for charging fees
- resolving ethical conflict
- acceptance of gifts
- dealing with threats to independence
- identifying procedures for whistle-blowing
- procedures for taking on new clients

Suggested time allocation: three hours

SIMULATION 1
CLARKE HOMER

SITUATION

You are an Accounting Technician employed by Clarke Homer, a firm of accountants based in Roundridge. You have responsibility for a number of clients and although you have to report to one of the partners you have prime responsibility for the day-to-day contact with your clients.

The tasks you have been asked to complete are set out below.

TASKS

Task 1

Read the information for Task 1 on page 142.

(a)   Bearing in mind the problems caused by the conduct of Steve Johns, the senior partner has asked you to prepare a brief presentation on the principles of professional ethics for the next staff meeting.

Use pages 143-144 to prepare some notes for this meeting, explaining the following six principles:

- Confidentiality
- Integrity
- Objectivity
- Due Care
- Professional and technical competence
- Professional behaviour

(b)   On page 145 identify and describe the ethical issues that are raised by the behaviour of the junior member of staff.

You should allow 30 minutes to complete this task

Task 2

Keira, a friend of yours who is also a member of the AAT has just separated from her husband who is also an accountant. She asks for your advice. Keira currently works for the practice that her husband owns but is now talking about setting up in practice with another accountant, and wonders if you are interested in joining her in this venture.

Keira states that if the two of you set up together she will be able to get clients from her husband's firm as she has all the details of her clients saved on disk. She has suggested that you may be able to do the same with clients from the firm that you work for.

Keira would like to name the new firm 'Profits R Us' and suggests that the advertising strategy should be very aggressive and include the following:

■   The firm will offer a 20% reduction on fees in the first year to all new clients.

■   Any clients from either of your current firms who transfers to the new firm will receive a 40% reduction on their first year's fees.

■   Existing clients will receive a commission payment for any new clients that they introduce.

■   Leaflets should be designed, pointing out:

–   Profits R Us will give a much better service than any other local firms.

–   Profits R Us will be much cheaper than other local accountants.

–   Profits R Us will guarantee to reduce any client's tax bill by at least 10% or the firm will pay the difference back to the client.

(a)   Use page 146 to explain whether it would be ethically correct for you and your friend to set up in business together using her suggestions to obtain clients from both your current firms.

(b)   Analyse the suggestions your friend has made for advertising the new firm and use pages 146-147 to comment on whether each of these suggestions is ethically appropriate for advertising a firm of accountants.

You should allow 20 minutes to complete this task

Task 3

After a few days off work you come back to the office to find a letter from a local employment agency. The letter asks you to supply the following information for a client of yours who is planning to use temporary staff supplied by the agency.

■   Financial Statements for the last two years

■   the latest Management Accounts

■   details of the client's current borrowings

Use page 148 to explain how you would deal with this request.

You should allow 10 minutes to complete this task

Task 4

You have a meeting arranged with your senior partner to discuss a new client, Estrapack Limited, that he has recently obtained for the firm, and would like you to manage.

The client's main business is importing speciality food from all over the world. The work for the client will involve the preparation of complex and detailed VAT calculations as well as the preparation of monthly management accounts.

You have a wide range of accounting experience but have not done any VAT work since your AAT studies.

(a)   Use page 149 to set out notes for your meeting with the partner, stating whether or not you consider you are able to take on this client.

(b)   Use page 149 to set out six appropriate ways for a member of the AAT to obtain the required amount of Continuing Professional Development (CPD).

You should allow 25 minutes to complete this task

Task 5

You hold a meeting with a new client you have just taken on. After some introductory chat he produces a large number of £50 notes in an envelope from his case and asks if you would hold on to the money for him so that it will be available to pay his tax bill in three months time.

He says 'I reckon there's about £10,000 here, which should do the job.'

Use page 150 to set out:

(a)   The points you should consider before agreeing to look after the money for the client.

(b)   The key procedures that should be in place for holding client money.

You should allow 20 minutes to complete this task

Task 6

At a meeting with a potential client the subject turns to the fees that you are going to charge. There are two elements to the work that you may be asked to carry out:

■   a one-off project to prepare a business plan to support a loan application to the bank

■   the preparation of the client's annual accounts

The client suggests that the fee for the preparation of the business plan should be contingent on the success or failure of the loan application.

He would also like you to explain the normal basis on which your fees are calculated for accountancy work.

He also says that his firm will not make a decision as to whether to employ you to prepare their annual accounts until after the bank has made its decision about the loan application. The implication here is that the work on the annual accounts is also contingent on the success of the loan application.

On pages 151-152:

(a)   State, giving reasons, whether you can accept the assignment to prepare the loan application for the bank on a contingent basis.

(b)   Explain the normal basis on which fees would be calculated for an accountancy assignment such as the preparation of the annual accounts.

(c)   Outline the key points that should be included in a letter of engagement sent to a new client.

You should allow 20 minutes to complete this task.

Task 7

One of the clients that you are responsible for is Enduring Health, a private health and fitness club in Roundridge. The fitness club has been one of your clients for a number of years and you have a good working relationship with the staff there.

When you are reviewing the files for the current year you notice the following issues:

■   The bookkeeper appears to have taken some money out of the health club and treated it as a loan in the accounts of the business.

■   There appears to be a discrepancy between the amount of VAT that should have been paid to HMRC compared with the amount that was paid, however you are not a VAT expert.

■   there is a note attached to the file addressed to you offering you free membership of the club.

Set out the ethical issues that arise from each of these three points on pages 152 to 153 and explain the possible courses of action open to you.

You should allow 15 minutes to complete this task.

Task 8

Your brother has recently set up in business as a personal trainer and nutritionist. Over a family meal he tells you that business is going well and that he has recently approached Enduring Health (see Task 7) to offer his services as a consultant. He goes on to say that they are interested in his services and need him to produce a detailed business proposal. He then asks you if you would help him to prepare the financial elements of the plan.

On page 154 explain whether you should agree to your brother's request. Give reasons for your answer.

You should allow 10 minutes to complete this task

Task 9

You are out on an assignment at Gateway Engineering Ltd, one of your long-standing clients.

A line manager approaches you and asks if he could have a quiet chat. He explains to you that he is very concerned about some of the things that are going on in the factory. In particular he believes that the company is breaking Health & Safety Regulations on some of the production lines in an attempt to cut costs. He says that he had intended to raise this issue with his bosses, but the last person who did so was sacked for some very minor reason.

He has heard that he may get some legal protection if he decides to 'blow the whistle' on his employer, but is unsure of the details of how he should go about this.

Use page 155 to set out the points he should consider when deciding whether to 'blow the whistle' on the company.

You should allow 15 minutes to complete this task

Task 10

Reach Out Limited is a client which operates a local coach company. It has recently taken over another coach business called On Tour Limited.

Reach Out has decided to rename the purchased company 'Continuous Travel Limited' and they want your firm to become the accountants for this new acquisition.

Using page 156 to explain:

(a)   the appropriate procedures for obtaining information from On Tour's previous accountants

(b)   the necessary administrative points that should be covered before Continuous Travel Limited can be taken on as a new client.

You should allow 15 minutes to complete this task

INFORMATION FOR TASK 1

As part of his responsibilities, Steve Johns, a junior member of staff sometimes has to sit at the reception desk whilst carrying out his work in case any clients or members of the public come into the office. On a number of occasions he has left client files unattended in the public area. He has also been heard discussing with clients the work that he has performed for other clients, often exaggerating the importance of the tasks that he has carried out.

Steve is very keen to progress within the firm and often tries to carry out tasks for which he has not been trained. In these circumstances he relies on his own ability and rarely asks for advice. He tends to work quickly and often makes mistakes.

ANSWER PAGES

Task 1 (a)

PRINCIPLE	EXPLANATION
confidentiality	
integrity	
objectivity	

continued . . .

PRINCIPLE	EXPLANATION
due care	
professional and technical competence	
professional behaviour	

Task 1 (b)

Task 2 (a)

Task 2 (b)

SUGGESTION	YOUR COMMENT
the name 'Profits-R-Us'	

SUGGESTION	YOUR COMMENT
20% reduction in first year's fees for new clients	
40% reduction in first year's fees for existing clients transferring	
commission payment to existing clients for introducing new clients	
LEAFLET DROP • **how much better the service than other firms**	
• **how much cheaper than other local firms**	
• **guarantee to reduce the client's tax bill by 10% or pay the difference**	

Task 3

Task 4 (a)

Task 4 (b)

1

2

3

4

5

6

Task 5 (a)

Task 5 (b)

Task 6 (a)

Task 6 (b)

Task 6 (c)

Task 7

ETHICAL ISSUE	PROPOSED ACTION
bookkeeper's loan	**bookkeeper's loan**

ETHICAL ISSUE	PROPOSED ACTION
VAT discrepancy	**VAT discrepancy**
free health club membership	**free health club membership**

Task 8

Task 9

Task 10 (a)

Task 10 (b)

Unit 32
Professional Ethics

Simulation 2: Abel, Ahmed & Toms
(adapted from AAT sample material) © AAT, 2005

Element coverage

32.1   Apply general principles and procedures for ethical compliance expected within the accounting sector.

32.2   Develop, maintain and apply ethics in employer/employee situations.

32.3   Develop, maintain and apply ethics in public practice.

Scenario and contents

This Simulation is based on Abel, Ahmed & Toms, a firm of accountants in public practice. You are an Accounting Technician employed by this firm. The tasks relate to:

- the identification of ethical principles
- ethical implications of receiving gifts and benefits from clients
- implications of client fraud and breach of legal requirements
- ethical issues in the completion of expenses claims and time sheets
- ethical principles relating to client confidentiality
- the need for technical expertise and the importance of CPD
- ethical implications of advisory services
- technicalities of changing accountants
- identification of ethical principles
- the charging of contingent fees
- the ethics of marketing methods used in promoting accountancy services

Suggested time allocation: three hours

SIMULATION 2
ABEL, AHMED & TOMS

SITUATION

You are an Accounting Technician employed by Abel Ahmed & Toms, a firm of accountants based in Aberdovey. You have responsibility for several clients, reporting to a partner who oversees your work, but you are the main contact for the clients.

The tasks you have been asked to complete are set out below.

There is additional background information on pages 162-163.

TASKS

Task 1

You have been asked to present a training session on professional ethics to some new trainees at your firm.

(a) Use pages 164-165 to give a brief explanation of what is meant by each of the following.

- Confidentiality

- Honesty and integrity

- Independence and objectivity

- Professional and technical competence

- Professional behaviour

- Due care

(b) Read the 'client background information' and the 'personal matters' given on pages 162-163, and set out on pages 166-167 the ways in which you can use these situations to demonstrate ethical issues that arise in everyday practice.

You should allow 40 minutes to complete this task.

Task 2

During your presentation one of the trainees makes the following comment.

"One of the reasons I wanted to get into accountancy was because I've heard you can get some really good deals from clients – I have a friend who even got a holiday because the client was so pleased with what he did for them."

Use page 168 to set out your response to this remark.

You should allow 10 minutes to complete this task.

Task 3

Another trainee who is present at your presentation starts to tell everyone about the company where he previously worked.

He explains how they used to pay people beneath the minimum wage, and how he had to pay people for a certain number of hours so that they would be entitled to state benefit, and made the rest up in cash.

He also started to talk about the fact that the company didn't comply with regulations regarding the use of the machinery in the work place.

Use page 169 to set out how you could use what he is saying to illustrate some ethical issues.

You should allow 10 minutes to complete this task.

Task 4

At the end of your training session it has been decided that you should include a session on claiming expenses and completing time sheets.

Use page 170 to set out why is it appropriate to include this in an ethics training session.

Your should allow 10 minutes to complete this task.

Task 5

Having completed your training session you return to you desk to find a fax from a lending institution asking for financial information about one of your clients. The fax asks for an immediate response to enable the finance to be arranged as soon as possible. This is the first you have heard of this.

Use page 171 to set out the ethical issues which arise in this situation.

You should allow 10 minutes to complete this task.

Task 6

Your art gallery client (see background information on page 163) has asked for some very specific advice on VAT issues. You know a bit about this, but have not dealt with it for thee years and are not totally confident that you will give the right information. The client does not want to pay for this extra advice as she considers it should be part of the whole service.

Use page 172 to describe the way in which you should deal with this situation and the issues that it raises.

You should allow 15 minutes to complete this task.

Task 7

In the evening you go to a local restaurant and, by chance, meet a client of the firm. He asks you several questions about inheritance tax and capital gains tax and then mentions that he has just come into quite a large sum of money and asks you to give him some advice on what would be the best thing to do with it.

Use page 173 to set out how you would respond to these questions, highlighting the ethical issues that come out of this.

You should allow 10 minutes to complete this task.

Task 8

(a)   You are conducting a meeting with a potential client.

Use page 174 to set out how you respond to the following questions:

-     How much will you charge?

-     How do I get the information from my previous accountant?

-     A friend of mine said his accountant would not release any information once he changed accountants, are they allowed to do that?

-     I would like you to hold some money on my behalf for reasons that I would rather not discuss. Can you do this for me?

-     The sign of a good accountants is the amount of tax he or she saves you. How much tax do you think you will be able to save me?

(b)   Later in the day you receive a telephone call from the potential client saying that he would like to change to your firm but he asks you not to write to his previous accountants. He says he will get all the information you require.

Use page 175 to set out what you should do in this situation.

You should allow 35 minutes to complete this task.

Task 9

You receive a telephone call from an existing client asking you to prepare a funding proposal to assist in raising finance for their business. He says this is very urgent and would like you to start work on it straightaway, but he asks that your fee be dependent on the success or otherwise in raising finance.

The client has specifically stated that it is only the proposal which he requires from you and will not need any further help with the raising of the money.

Set out on page 176 the matters that need to be agreed before you start work including whether his suggestion regarding the fee is acceptable.

You should allow 10 minutes to complete this task.

Task 10

Your firm has decided to launch a new marketing campaign with the aim of increasing the number of clients and the fee income. The partners have asked for suggestions from all employees for ways of gaining new clients.

Some of the suggestions are set out below:

- point out how much lower our fees are than the other local firms

- point out that we give a better service than the other local firms

- offer a 25% discount for the first year to all new clients

- offer a commission to all staff for any clients introduced to the firm

- when new employees join the firm from another practice, give them an extra incentive to bring clients from their old firm with them

- offer a free initial consultation for every potential client

- offer commission to existing clients for any new clients they introduce

Use the table on pages 177 to 178 to comment on how appropriate these suggestions are in relation to professional ethics.

You should allow 30 minutes to complete this task.

CLIENT BACKGROUND INFORMATION

Boat builders

This client is a limited company owned by a father and son. The company owns a property of relatively high value which was purchased three years ago and has since significantly increased in value. The property is now on the market as the company is struggling financially and needs to sell it quickly.

The son, who has the boat building expertise, wishes to leave to do other things. The father and son have fallen out over the exit route for the son and you are trying to mediate.

Over the years you have acted for them you have formed a good relationship with the son, but have always found the father difficult to talk to, and he shows little interest in or understanding of the financial aspects of the business. The son is planning to go into partnership in a new venture outside the area but he has said he would very much like you to continue to act for him. His ability to buy into the new venture depends a great deal on the settlement from the existing family business.

In passing you have heard the son say that he does not invoice for all jobs and puts the money straight into his personal account.

You have also been told that there is one employee who is not on the payroll and is paid in cash. He is particularly skilful and would be difficult to replace, and he will not work unless he is paid in this way.

Care home

This is a care home for old people run by a married couple who happen to live in the same road as you do.

The maintenance of the road you live in is the joint responsibility of the residents. The road has recently been maintained, and you are all supposed to be sharing the cost. However, the owner of the care home arranged for the work to be done and you know that he had similar work carried out at the care home at the same time. You have asked him for a copy of the invoice for your own records, and although you have paid him, he keeps finding reasons not to show you the invoice. You therefore are beginning to suspect that the total cost will be put through as a business expense.

From looking at the books of the boat builders (above) you know that the husband has recently had a boat built. This is common knowledge, but his wife has told you that he has spent £1,000 on this, whereas you know from the boat builders records that the boat cost £3,000.

This week you are preparing quarterly management accounts for the care home and you notice a 'boat builder' invoice in amongst repairs and maintenance which has been described as 'welding work', it is for £3,000.

The care home has a residential flat above it which the clients let out. When preparing their tax return, they say they have not let it out for the whole year, but there is something in the way he says it which makes you think this may not be true.

Property developer

You have a meeting arranged with a local property developer. He wants to discuss plans for future investments and he has asked you to bring along ideas for potential properties. He is always interested in getting a good deal and tends to let people hang on until they are desperate to sell.

He lets one of his properties out to another client of yours who runs an art gallery (see next page). The developer has told you that he plans to sell very soon.

Art gallery

Your clients have been talking about their long term plans for their gallery and how their present location is ideally suited to their plans. They are thinking about investing a large amount of money in changing the premises to the way they need it for their business and are currently spending a lot of time on planning this at the expense of their existing business.

A personal friend of yours exhibits at the gallery and is paid a commission for any sales made. From the work you have done on the accounts it appears that the gallery have been taking prints of your friend's pictures and selling them without her knowledge.

PERSONAL MATTERS

Your friend

Your friend also has a gallery in the town and she has told you that she is 'letting' some space to a client of yours who is a VAT registered sole trader. Your friend says he is trying to break into the art world and has been quite successful in selling some of his paintings. His accounts, which you prepare quarterly, show no income from this source.

Your brother in law

Your brother in law has recently been offered a job with one of your larger clients. He and your sister are very excited and see it as a major career move; the additional money he will be earning will enable them to start a family and buy a larger house.

You were aware that your client was looking to recruit, but the level of pay that your brother in law has been told is far higher than the figure you had been given by your client.

The last set of accounts you prepared for the company were qualified on a going concern basis and you know the company has serious financial difficulties.

Your house

You are having an extension built by a local builder who is not a client. This is completely outside your professional work. He offers to do the build for cash so that you don't have to pay VAT.

ANSWER PAGES

Task 1 (a)

PRINCIPLE	EXPLANATION
confidentiality	
honesty and integrity	
independence and objectivity	

PRINCIPLE	EXPLANATION
professional and technical competence	
professional behaviour	
due care	

Task 1 (b)

Boat builders

Care home

Art gallery

Your friend

Your brother-in-law

Your house

Task 2

Task 3

Task 4

Task 5

Task 6

Task 7

Task 8 (a)

Client question/comment	Your response
How much will you charge?	
How do I get information from my previous accountant?	
A friend of mine said his accountant would not release any information once he had changed accountants. Are they allowed to do that?	
I would like you to hold some money on my behalf for reasons that I would rather not discuss. Can you do this for me?	
The sign of a good accountant is how much tax they can save you. How much tax do you think you will be able to save me?	

Task 8 (b)

Task 9

Task 10

SUGGESTION	YOUR COMMENT
Point out how much lower our fees are than those of other local firms.	
Point out that we give a better service than other local firms.	
Offer a 25% discount for the first year to all new clients.	
Offer a commission to all staff for any clients introduced to the firm.	

SUGGESTION	YOUR COMMENT
When new employees join the firm from another practice, give them an extra incentive to bring clients from their old firm with them.	
Offer a free initial consultation for every potential client.	
Offer a commission to existing clients for any new clients they introduce to the firm.	

Appendix 1

AAT Guidelines on Professional Ethics

1. Introduction

1.1   These guidelines on Professional Ethics are applicable to all fellow, full, affiliate and student members and unless otherwise indicated, the term 'member' used for the purposes of the Guidelines, is deemed to include affiliates and student members. The Guidelines were revised in 1999, and approved by the AAT Council, to come into effect on 1 January 2000.

1.2   The guidelines are based on the principles set out in the Code of Ethics for Professional Accountants approved by the International Federation of Accountants (IFAC) in January 1998, supplemented where appropriate by guidance of specific relevance to AAT members. The Guidelines are in three parts:

- The first part (Sections 1 to 3) applies to all members;

- The second part (Section 4) represents additional guidance which applies specifically to employed members, including in appropriate circumstances, members employed in public practice;

- The third part (Sections 5 and 6) applies specifically to the members in practice. Members in practice in the UK are required to register annually with the AAT in accordance with the scheme for members in practice.

1.3   In certain of the Guidelines reference is made to issues which are essentially legal in nature. The law cited is that of the United Kingdom. Members overseas should seek appropriate advice as to the relevant legal situation within their own countries. In particular, the guidelines in Section 6 seek to provide helpful advice on legal situations which may arise, particularly in relation to the activities of members in practice in the UK. They do not purport to be definitive legal advice for every situation. Members who encounter problems in relation to legal aspects are recommended to seek the advice of their solicitor. Where guidelines are based on UK law, members are expected to comply with these as a minimum requirement as a matter of good practice. In addition, members are expected to know and apply the laws of the country in which they work or live, having taken local legal advice if necessary.

1.4   Reference is also made in the guidelines to aspects of the regulatory regime of the AAT.

1.5   There may be occasions when members, whether having sought independent advice or not, and having considered the application of the ethical guidelines in a particular situation, are still in doubt about the proper course of action to be taken. In such cases they should contact the Ethics Advice line on tel: 020 7415 7619 giving all the relevant facts.

1.6   The accountancy profession, including the part represented by the AAT, is committed to the following objectives:

(i)   Mastering of particular skills and techniques acquired through learning and education and maintained through continuing professional development;

(ii)   Development of an ethical approach to the work and to employers and clients, acquired by experience and professional supervision under training and safeguarded by a strict ethical and disciplinary code;

(iii) Acknowledgement of duties to society as a whole in addition to duties to the employer or the client;

(iv) An outlook which is essentially objective, obtained by being fair minded and free from conflicts of interest (see section 3.1.1);

(v) Rendering personal services to the highest standards of conduct and performance;

(vi) Achieving acceptance by the public that members provide accountancy services in accordance with these high standards and requirements.

The Guidelines aim to assist members to achieve these objectives.

2. Fundamental principles

All members should observe certain fundamental principles in order to achieve the objectives of the profession:

2.1 Integrity

Members should be straightforward and honest in performing professional work.

2.2 Objectivity

Members should be fair and should not allow prejudice or bias or the influence of others to override objectivity.

2. 3 Professional and technical competence

2.3.1 Members should refrain from undertaking or continuing any assignments which they are not competent to carry out unless advice and assistance is obtained to ensure that the assignment is carried out satisfactorily.

2.3.2 Members also have a continuing duty:

(i) to maintain professional knowledge and skill at a level required to ensure that a client or employer receives the advantage of competent professional service based on up-to-date developments in practice, legislation and techniques;

(ii) to maintain their technical and ethical standards in areas relevant to their work through continuing professional development.

2.4 Due care

2.4.1 A member, having accepted an assignment, has an obligation to carry it out with due care and reasonable despatch having regard to the nature and scope of the assignment.

2.4.2 Special care is required where members undertake assignments for clients who may have little or no knowledge of accounting and taxation matters.

2.5 Confidentiality

Members should respect the confidentiality of information acquired during the course of performing professional work and should not use or disclose any such information without proper and specific authority or unless there is a legal or professional right or duty to disclose.

2.6 Professional behaviour

Members should act in a manner consistent with the good reputation of the profession and refrain from any conduct which might bring discredit to the profession.

2.7 The fundamental principles

The fundamental principles are of a general nature. They do not generally solve members' ethical problems in specific cases. Therefore, the ethical guidelines which follow also provide detailed guidance on the application in practice of the objectives and the application of the fundamental principles in a number of typical situations occurring in the accountancy profession.

3. Guidance applicable to all members

3.1 Objectivity

3.1.1 Section 1 of the guidelines emphasises the need for a member to maintain objectivity at all times. The principle of objectivity imposes the obligation on all members to be fair minded, intellectually honest and free from conflicts of interest.

3.1.2 Members serve in many different capacities and should demonstrate their objectivity in varying circumstances. Members in practice undertake professional services. Other members as employees prepare financial statements, perform internal audit services and serve in financial management capacities in the accountancy profession, industry, commerce, public sector and education. Members also educate and train those who aspire to admission to the AAT.

3.1.3 Regardless of service or capacity, members should protect the integrity of their professional services, maintain objectivity and avoid any subordination of their judgement by others.

3.1.4 Members need to bear in mind, in this context, the following factors:

(i) Whatever the nature of the professional services they provide, members may be exposed to situations which involve the possibility of pressures and threats being exerted on them. These pressures and threats may impair their objectivity, and hence their independence;

(ii) In dealing with independence, members must address both:

■ independence of mind, ie. the state of mind which has regard to all considerations relevant to the task in hand but no other – independence of mind is also referred to as objectivity;

■ independence in appearance, (or independence that can be demonstrated) ie. the avoidance of situations inducing so obvious a threat to independence that an informed third party would question the member's objectivity. Issues of independence in appearance are most likely to arise in relation to undertaking audit or other public financial reporting assignments. These aspects are dealt with in Section 5.2;

(iii) In situations which do not necessarily require independence in appearance, members are generally able to safeguard their objectivity by analysing the threats and pressures which arise, and weighing against them the acknowledged safeguards which may be employed to negate those threats and pressures or reduce them to acceptable levels. Many safeguards arise as a result of:

■ a member's normal strength of character and professionalism which enables him or her to confront the threats and pressures which may be exerted on him or her by employers or clients;

■ the fear of pressures of legal accountability;

■ the possibility of professional discipline and enforcement; and

■ the loss of reputation.

(iv) Members have an obligation to ensure that personnel engaged in professional work are aware of the need to preserve their objectivity and, where appropriate, to demonstrate their independence.

3.1.5 Acceptance of gifts etc.

Objectivity may be threatened or appear to be threatened by the acceptance by a member, or the spouse or dependent children of a member, of gifts, services, favours or hospitality from a client, or, in the case of an employed member, from a work colleague or a person having or proposing to have a contractual relationship with the member's employer.

Employed members should be aware of the difficulties which may arise from the offer or the acceptance of any gift, service, favour or hospitality which may be intended to influence the recipient or which could be interpreted by a reasonable person in full possession of the facts as likely to have that effect. The attention of members serving in UK government, local and public authorities, or other public bodies is particularly drawn to the provisions of the Public Bodies Corrupt Practices Act 1889 and the Prevention of Corruption Acts 1906/16, and any other Acts of relevance to public service which remain in force.

3.2 Presentation of information

3.2.1 A member is expected to present financial information fully, honestly and professionally and so that it will be understood in its context.

3.2.2 Financial information should describe clearly the true nature of business transactions, assets and liabilities. It should classify and record entries in a timely and proper manner. Members should do everything that is within their powers to ensure that this is the case, and in particular that such information is in accordance with accepted accounting standards.

3.3 Resolution of Ethical Conflicts

3.3.1 From time to time members may encounter situations which give rise to ethical conflicts. Such conflicts may arise in a wide variety of ways, ranging from the relatively trivial dilemma to the extreme case of fraud and similar illegal activities. If members are instructed or encouraged to engage in any activity which is unlawful they are entitled and required to decline. For example, members should not be party to the falsification of any record or knowingly or recklessly supply any information or make any statement which is misleading, false or deceptive.

3.3.2 If the member would feel uncomfortable defending an action in open court or to the press then it is likely that such a course of action should be avoided on ethical grounds.

3.3.3 An honest difference of opinion between a member and another person is not itself an ethical issue.

3.3.4 In resolving ethical conflicts the member should consider seeking counselling and advice on a confidential basis with an independent legal advisor and/or the Ethics Advice line on tel: 020 7415 7619.

3.3.5 It is important to keep a written record of all meetings and discussions which take place in seeking to resolve an ethical conflict.

3.3.6 For guidance on Conflict of Loyalties affecting employed members, see Section 4.2 and for members in practice, see Section 5.2.

3.4 Professional competence

3.4.1 Members should refrain from undertaking or continuing assignments which they are not competent to carry out, unless competent advice and assistance is obtained to enable them satisfactorily to carry out the assignment.

3.4.2 A member's professional competence may be divided into two separate phases:

(i) Attainment of professional competence

The attainment of professional competence requires specific education, training, assessment or examination in professionally relevant subjects and, whether prescribed or not, a period of relevant work experience in finance or accountancy;

(ii) Maintenance of professional competence

(a) The maintenance of professional competence requires a continuing awareness and application of developments in the accountancy profession including relevant national and international pronouncements on accounting, auditing and other relevant regulations and statutory requirements. To achieve this, Council has recommended a programme of a minimum of 60 hours of relevant CPD over 2 years with at least 20 hours in any single year. Members in practice should also refer to paragraph 5.1 for CPD requirements.

(b) Members should adopt review procedures that will ensure the quality of their professional work is consistent with national and international pronouncements that are issued from time to time.

3.4.3 The guidance in paragraph 3.4.2 is applicable to student members only to the extent that it is compatible with the stage they have reached in their training and work experience.

3.5 Confidentiality

3.5.1 Members have an obligation to respect the confidentiality of information about a client's or employer's affairs, or the affairs of clients of employers, acquired in the course of professional work. The duty of confidentiality continues even after the end of the relationship between the member and the employer or client.

3.5.2 Confidentiality should always be observed by members unless specific authority has been given to disclose information or there is a legal, regulatory or professional duty to disclose.

3.5.3 Members have an obligation to ensure that staff under their control and persons from whom advice and assistance is obtained respect the principle of confidentiality.

3.5.4 Confidentiality concerns the matter of usage of information and not just non-disclosure or disclosure. A member acquiring information in the course of professional work should neither use nor appear to use that information for personal advantage or for the advantage of a third party.

3.5.5 Members have access to much confidential information about an employer's or client's affairs, or the affairs of clients of employers, not otherwise disclosed to the public. Therefore members should be relied upon not to make unauthorised disclosures to other persons. This does not apply to disclosure of information in order to discharge their responsibilities properly according to the profession's standards.

3.5.6 The following are examples of the points which should be considered in determining the extent to which confidential information may be disclosed:

(i) When disclosure is authorised.

When authorisation to disclose is given by the client or the employer, the interests of all the parties including those third parties whose interests might be affected should be considered.

(ii) When disclosure is specifically required by law. This could lead to a member:

(a) producing documents or giving evidence in the course of legal proceedings; and

(b) disclosing to the appropriate public authorities infringements of the law. A particular example of the latter situation is in relation to money laundering. The Criminal Justice Act, 1993 requires, in relation to drugs or terrorist activities, that members report to the National Criminal Intelligence Service (NCIS) suspicions they have formed that they may be in danger of assisting a money launderer. In particular, the Act creates an offence of "tipping-off" the money launderer in such circumstances, the penalties for which are extremely severe. Further, firms engaged in relevant financial business (as defined by the Money Laundering Regulations) including those authorised under the Financial Services Act, are required to establish specific procedures for the identification and prevention of money laundering. All the countries of the European Union, and many other countries outside it, have anti-money laundering legal provisions.

(iii) Where there is a professional duty

(a) to comply with technical standards and ethical requirements;

(b) to protect the professional interests of the member in legal proceedings;

(c) to respond to an enquiry by the AAT or by a regulatory body of an ethical, investigatory or disciplinary nature.

3.5.7 When the member has determined that confidential information can be disclosed, the following points should be considered.

- whether or not all the relevant facts are known and substantiated, to the extent it is practicable to do so; when the situation involves unsubstantiated fact or opinion, professional judgement should be used in determining the type of disclosure to be made, if any;

■ what type of communication is expected and to whom it will be communicated; in particular, the member should be satisfied that the parties to whom the communication is addressed are appropriate recipients and have the authority to act on it; and

■ whether or not the member would incur any legal liability having made a communication and the consequences of incurring the relevant legal liability.

In all such situations, the member should consider the need to take advice from a solicitor. See also paragraph 4.2.5, with reference to the Public Interest Disclosure Act.

3.6 Taxation services

3.6.1 Members performing taxation services in the UK, Ireland and in other member states of the EU will be dealing with compliance and advice on Value Added Tax – an indirect tax and direct taxes based on income, gains, losses and profits. The administrative authorities and the legal basis for direct and indirect taxes differ substantially and are detailed.

3.6.2 It is beyond the scope of these guidelines to deal with detailed ethical issues relating to taxation services encountered by members. The Ethics Advice line on tel: 020 7415 7619 will give assistance to members seeking advice in the UK by referring to the extensive ethical guides of the Sponsoring Bodies which deal with taxation. Reference will also be made to those statements of the Chartered Institute of Taxation which have been cleared with the Commissioners of Inland Revenue and Customs and Excise as appropriate and to Technical Release TAX 15/97 of the Institute of Chartered Accountants in England and Wales.

3.6.3 The guidance that follows consists therefore of general principles for members which apply to both direct and indirect taxation.

3.6.4 A member providing professional tax services has a duty to put forward the best position in favour of a client or an employer. However, the service must be carried out with professional competence, must not in any way impair integrity or objectivity, and must be consistent with the law.

3.6.5 A member should not hold out to a client or an employer the assurance that any tax return prepared and tax advice offered are beyond challenge. Instead the member should ensure that the client or the employer is aware of the limitations attaching to tax advice and services so that they do not misinterpret an expression of opinion as an assertion of fact.

3.6.6 A member should only undertake taxation work on the basis of full disclosure by the client or employer. The member, in dealing with the tax authorities, must act in good faith, and exercise care in relation to facts or information presented on behalf of the client or employer. It will normally be assumed that facts and information on which business tax computations are based were provided by the client or employer as the taxpayer, and the latter bears ultimate responsibility for the accuracy of the facts, information and tax computations. The member should avoid assuming responsibility for the accuracy of facts, etc. outside his or her own knowledge.

3.6.7 When a member submits a tax return or tax computations for a taxpayer client or employer, the member is acting as an agent. The nature and responsibilities of the member's duties should be made clear to the client or employer, in the case of the former by an engagement letter (see Section 5.5).

3.6.8   Tax advice or opinions of material consequence given to a client or an employer should be recorded, either in the form of a letter or in a memorandum for the files.

3.6.9   A member should not be associated with any return or communication in which there is reason to believe that it:

(i)   contains a false or misleading statement;

(ii)   contains statements or information furnished recklessly or without any real knowledge of whether they are true or false; or

(iii)   omits or obscures information required to be submitted and such omission or obscurity would mislead the tax authorities.

3.6.10 In the case of a members in practice, acting for a client, the member should furnish copies of all tax computations to the client before submitting them to the Revenue.

3.6.11 When a member learns of a material error or omission in a tax return of a prior year, or f a failure to file a required tax return, the member has a responsibility to advise promptly the client or employer of the error or omission and recommend that disclosure be made to the Revenue (normally the member is not obliged to inform the Revenue, and should not do so without the permission of the client or employer).

If the client or employer does not correct the error, the member should inform the client or employer that it is not possible for the member to act for them in connection with that return or other related information submitted to the authorities.

3.6.12 In the case of a self-employed member whose client refuses to make disclosure of an error or omission to the Revenue, the member should cease to act for the client, informing the client, in writing, to that effect:

(i)   Where the member has acted in relation to the error or omission, he or she should also inform the Revenue that they have ceased to act, adding, if it is the case, that the member has received information indicating that accounts and statements, etc. should not be relied upon;

(ii)   However, where the member has not acted in relation to the error or omission, although the member should cease to act, his or her communication with the Revenue should be restricted to a bare notification to that effect.

3.6.13 The tax authorities in many countries have extensive powers to obtain information (in the UK this is primarily in the case of the Inland Revenue under the Taxes Management Act 1970, S.20/A/BC, and in the case of Customs under the VAT act 1994, Schedule 11). Members confronted by the exercise of those powers by the authorities should seek appropriate legal advice.

4.   Guidance applicable to employed members

4.1   Introduction

The following Sections contain guidance which is relevant to members employed in industry, commerce, the public sector, education or in public practice.

4.2   Conflict of Loyalties

4.2.1   Employed members owe a duty of loyalty to their employer as well as to their profession and there may be times when the two are in conflict. An employee's normal priority should be to support his or her organisation's legitimate and ethical objectives and the rules and procedures drawn up in support of them. However, an employee cannot legitimately be required to:

(i)   break the law;

(ii)   breach the rules and standards of their profession;

(iii) lie to or mislead (including by keeping silent) those acting as auditors to the employer; or

(iv)   put their name to or otherwise be associated with a statement which materially misrepresents the facts.

4.2.2   When members become aware that their employers have committed an unlawful act which could compromise them every effort should be made to persuade the employer not to perpetuate the unlawful activity, and to rectify the matter.

4.2.3   Differences in view about the correct judgement on accounting or ethical matters should normally be raised and resolved within the employee's organisation, initially with the employee's immediate superior, and possible thereafter, where disagreement about a significant ethical issue remains, with higher levels of management or non-executive directors.

4.2.4   If employed accountants cannot resolve any material issue involving a conflict between their employers and their professional requirements they may, after exhausting all other relevant possibilities, have no other recourse but to consider resignation. An employer may also be influenced in taking the right decision if it is made clear by the member that it will not be possible to continue as an employee if matters are not corrected. Employees should state their reasons for resignation to the employer but their duty of confidentiality normally precludes them from communicating the issue to others (unless legally or professionally required to do so).

4.2.5   Before resigning it is strongly recommended that members should obtain appropriate legal advice. The Public Interest Disclosure Act, 1998 gives protection, including protection from dismissal, to employees in the UK who disclose otherwise confidential information internally or to a prescribed regulator in good faith.

An employee in the UK making public disclosure is protected, where he or she makes the disclosure in good faith, and reasonably believes that the information disclosed is substantially true and that he or she would otherwise be victimised or the evidence concealed or destroyed, or where the concern has already been raised with the employer or prescribed regulator.

4.3   Support for professional colleagues

A member, particularly one having authority over others, should give due weight to the need for them to develop and hold their own judgement in accounting matters and should deal with differences of opinion in a professional way.

4.4 Professional competence

A member employed in industry, commerce, the public sector or education may be asked to undertake significant tasks for which he or she has not had sufficient specific training or experience. When undertaking such work the member should not mislead the employer as to the degree of expertise or experience he or she possesses, and where appropriate expert advice, assistance or training should be sought.

5. Guidance applicable to members in practice

5.1 Introduction

5.1.1 Members who provide accounting, taxation or related consultancy services on a self-employed basis in the UK must register on the scheme for members in practice and comply with the Guidelines and Regulations for members in practice. Although student and affiliate members (also full members who provide related self-employed services outside the UK) would not be required to register on the scheme, it is recommended that they comply with the Guidelines and Regulations relating to members in practice. In addition, they must abide by the Association's Guidelines on Professional Ethics.

5.1.2 Members, unless appropriately authorised by a regulatory body established under statutory authority, may not, inter alia, perform the following functions in the UK:

(i) External audit of UK limited companies and other prescribed organisations in accordance with the provisions of the Companies Acts;

(ii) External audit of other bodies which require the services of a registered auditor;

(iii) Activities subject to the provisions of the Financial Services Act 1986. These include the undertaking of investment business and the provision of corporate finance advice to clients;

(iv) Insolvency practice in accordance with the provisions of the Insolvency Act 1986.

5.2 Independence in financial reporting and similar roles

5.2.1 When undertaking a financial reporting assignment, a members in practice should be independent both in fact and appearance (see Section 3.1 – Objectivity – above).

5.2.2 In order to safeguard their independence, members contemplating any such assignment should consider certain matters before deciding whether to accept a new appointment, or whether to continue an existing appointment. These matters include the expectations of those directly affected by the work; the environment in which the work is to be conducted, including that within the member's practice and the profession; the threats to objectivity which may actually arise or may appear to arise because of any expectations and the environment; and the safeguards which can be put in place to offset the risks and threats.

5.2.3   The guidelines on objectivity (see Section 3.1) emphasise the need for the member to maintain objectivity at all times. This is particularly so in financial reporting, and similar roles. In general, members should be able to reach a proper and responsible decision whether or not to accept or continue an engagement based on a realistic assessment and weighing of the threats to objectivity which arise and of the generally accepted safeguards which may be employed to negate those threats to objectivity or to reduce them to acceptable proportions.

5.2.4   The potential threats to objectivity and hence independence can be categorised in various ways. In essence they may arise from involvement by a members in practice (or a close connection) in the client's affairs. These threats may be:

■   financial in nature ("self-interest" threats);

■   resulting from an executive, managerial, or operational involvement in the client's affairs and/or in the preparation of its accounts (a "self-review" threat);

■   arising from an emotional commitment to the client or its interest (such as to create a "familiarity" or an "intimidation" threat);

■   or from taking a strongly proactive stance on the client's behalf (an "advocacy" threat).

5.2.5   Where threats exist, members should always consider the use of safeguards and procedures which may negate or reduce them. In certain countries, safeguards or requirements are provided for by law or professional rules. In those cases, the member has to comply with the existing rules. Failure to comply with these rules leads to professional disciplinary proceedings. Safeguards and procedures might include:

(i)   educational and experience requirements for entry into the profession;

(ii)   Continuing professional development requirements;

(iii) policies and procedures intended to promote quality control of reporting engagements;

(iv)   external or internal review or a firm's quality control system;

(v)   arrangements to ensure that staff are adequately aware and empowered to communicate any issue of independence and objectivity that concerns them;

(vi)   where available, the involvement of an additional principal who did not take part in the conduct of the reporting assignment;

(vii) where possible consulting a third party such as a committee of independent directors, or a professional regulatory body;

(viii) where possible arrangements to reduce the risk of conflict by compartmentalising responsibilities and knowledge in specific cases;

(ix)   where possible rotation of senior personnel;

(x)   publicly visible steps, possibly including a public announcement, to explain how the risk of conflict is recognised and mitigated in a specific situation;

(xi)   refusal to perform the assignment where no other appropriate course can abate the perceived problem.

5.2.6   Financial Involvement with or in the affairs of clients

Financial involvement with a client creates a self-interest threat to objectivity which is generally regarded as insurmountable. Financial involvement can arise in a number of ways, such as:

(i)   by direct or indirect financial interest

(ii)   by loans to or from the client or any officer, director or principal shareholder of a client company. The self-interest threat arising from outstanding fees is exacerbated when they become equivalent to a loan and a member should review the propriety of continuing to act where significant fees have been outstanding for twelve months or more. Special considerations may apply in circumstances involving Individual Voluntary Arrangements (IVAs) or other specific arrangements for payment;

(iii)   by holding a financial interest in a joint venture with a client or employee(s) or a client;

(iv)   when the receipt of fees from a client or group of connected clients represents a large proportion of the total gross fees of a member or of the practice as a whole. The perceived threat grows with the size of the fees and is thus increased by work or services additional to the reporting assignment;

(v)   the provision of other services may also give rise to self-review, familiarity, or advocacy threats (see paragraph 5.2.8).

5.2.7   Appointments in companies

When a member who is in practice is or was, within a period or two years prior to a potential assignment:

(i)   a member of the Board, an officer or employee or a company; or

(ii)   a partner of, or in the employment of, a member of the Board, or an officer or employee of a company;

then the member would be regarded as being subject to an insurmountable threat of a self-review nature, which would be incompatible with his or her continuing with a financial reporting assignment in relation to the company.

5.2.8   Provision of other services to clients

When members provide consultancy services to clients, care should be taken when rendering advice not to report on management decisions which the member has recommended, so as to avoid a self-review threat. The services provided by a self-employed member in the fields of management consultancy and taxation are advisory services which should not usurp the management functions of clients. Objectivity is not impaired by offering advisory services provided there is no involvement in, or responsibility assumed for, management decisions. Nevertheless, members should remain aware of a possible self-review threat, and be careful not to go beyond, or appear to go beyond the advisory function into the management sphere.

5.2.9   Personal and family relationships

Personal and family relationships can affect objectivity. There is a particular need to ensure that an objective approach to any assignment is not endangered as a consequence of any personal or family relationship. Family relationships which will normally impose an unacceptable threat to objectivity in relation to financial reporting assignments are those in which the member is the spouse, dependant child or relative living in a common household, of the client, or vice-versa.

5.2.10 Conflicts between interests or different clients

There is, on the face of it, nothing improper in a member or practice having two or more clients whose interests may be in conflict. In such a case however the work should be managed so as to avoid the interest of one client adversely affecting that of another. Where the acceptance or continuance of an engagement would, even with safeguards, materially prejudice the interests of any client the appointment should not be accepted or continued, or one of the appointments should be discontinued. All reasonable steps should be taken to ascertain whether any conflict of interest exists or is likely to arise, both in regard to new engagements and to any change in the circumstances of existing clients. Relationships with existing clients need to be considered before new appointments are considered. Wherever a significant conflict between the interests of different clients or potential clients is identified, sufficient disclosure should be made to both parties so that they may make an informed decision on whether to engage or continue their relationship with the member or practice.

5.3 Agencies

The following guidance refers mainly to building society agencies but the principles stated apply also, so far as they are relevant, to other forms of agency.

5.3.1 The acceptance by a member of any agency may present a threat to professional independence. Particular problems occur with building society agencies because of the expansion of their range of services beyond deposit and similar business to the inclusion of insurance and unit trust investments. Members in the UK should note that involvement in such business requires authorisation under the Financial Services Act 1986. A member who is not authorised under the Act may, however, act as a 'bare introducer', ie. refer an enquirer to, for example a list of providers of financial services, provided that the member gives no recommendation of any kind.

5.3.2 Before accepting an agency from a building society or other body, members should be satisfied:

(i)   that their professional independence will not be compromised;

(ii) that acceptance will not be rendered inappropriate by the nature of the services they are to provide or the manner in which those services may be brought to the attention of the public.

5.3.3 Although a member's operation of a building society agency restricted to simple forms of deposit taking would not require authorisation under the Financial Services Act 1986, the mere presence of agency signs and literature, together with the public perception of the increasing range of building society products and services, could produce a real danger that the member might be perceived to be carrying on investment business. Should an unauthorised UK member actually engage in investment business as defined by the Financial Services Act, that member could be committing a criminal offence.

5.3.4 For these reasons it will in normal circumstances be inappropriate for members, unless authorised, to enter into or continue any form of agency or other arrangement with a building society.

5.4   Commission

A member who receives a commission or other reward in return for the introduction of a client should be aware that if such an introduction is made in the course of a "fiduciary relationship" with the client, the member will be accountable for the commission or reward to the client. That means that the member will, under UK and other common law regimes, be bound to pass over the commission or reward to the client, unless the latter, having been informed of the nature and amount of the commission or reward, agrees that the member can keep it. A "fiduciary relationship" between a member and his or her client will arise:

- where the accountant acts as the client's agent; or

- where the accountant gives professional advice to the client so as to give rise to a relationship which the law would regard as one of "trust and confidence".

5.5   Letters of engagement

5.5.1   Members in practice should ensure that, as a matter of good practice, for each client an engagement letter is agreed. The purpose of such a letter is to provide written confirmation of the work to be undertaken and the extent of the member's responsibilities. Examples of letters of engagement are sent out automatically to those who email; Professional Standards@aat.org.uk and type as the subject heading: letterofengagement; or letterofengagementforcharities.

For telephone requests contact the Technical Manager.

The following features are recommended for inclusion:

(i)   The nature of the assignment.

The nature of the assignment, the scope of the work to be undertaken and, if appropriate the format and nature of any report which has to be delivered;

(ii)   Timing.

The timing of the engagement, ie. the date the work is expected to start, (and whether these dates are contingent on the completion by the client or others of information), the duration of the work and the dates on which reports are to be made;

(iii)   Duration.

Whether the assignment is monthly, annual or not recurring and whether the engagement will continue unless specifically terminated by the client;

(iv)   Client's responsibilities.

The client's responsibilities e.g. as to the production of information such as records and books, their format and timing. The client should also be advised that, for example, in relation to tax compliance work a member will only be acting as an agent for the client and that the client is responsible for the tax returns, etc. submitted;

(v) Detection of irregularities.

That the responsibility for the detection of irregularities and fraud rests with the client's management and this would normally be outside the scope of the engagement. Nevertheless it should be made clear, under the terms of the engagement letter that, the client is obliged to provide full information to the member;

(vi) Basis, frequency and rate of charge.

The basis, frequency and rate of charge for services rendered together with the treatment of expenses incurred in connection with the assignment. The incidence of any taxes should also be specified;

(vii) Ownership and lien.

The ownership of books and records created in the engagement and whether the member will exercise a lien over such items if fees remain unpaid or are disputed. The member's policy on retention, destruction and return of records should, if appropriate, be specified;

(viii) Unpaid fees.

The member's actions on a fee remaining unpaid after presentation of the invoice should be dealt with: including the charging of interest and at what rate, the cessation of work and, as above, the exercise of a lien over the client's books and records;

(ix) Third parties.

The usage of the member's work by the client for third parties should be specified and suitable disclaimers employed.

5.6 Fees and commissions

5.6.1 Members in public practice who undertake professional services for a client assume the responsibility to perform the work with integrity and objectivity and in accordance with the appropriate technical standards. That responsibility is discharged by applying the professional skill and knowledge which members have acquired and continue to acquire through learning and experience and which student members are in varying stages of acquiring. For the services rendered they are entitled to remuneration.

5.6.2 Professional fees should be a fair reflection of the value of the work performed for the client, taking into account:

(i) the skill and knowledge required for the type of work involved;

(ii) the level of training and experience of the persons necessarily engaged on the work;

(iii) the time necessarily occupied by each person engaged on the work; and

(iv) the degree of responsibility that the work entails.

5.6.3 Professional fees should normally be computed on the basis of agreed appropriate rates per hour of per day for the time of each person engaged on the work. These rates should be based on the fundamental premise that the organisation and conduct of the practice and the services provided to clients are well planned, controlled and managed.

5.6.4 A member should not make a representation that specific professional services in current or future periods will be performed for either a stated fee, estimated fee or fee range if it is likely at the time of the representation that such fees will be substantially increased and the prospective client is not advised of that likelihood.

5.6.5 When undertaking work for a client it may be necessary or expedient to charge a pre-arranged fee in which event the member should estimate a fee, taking into account the matters referred to in paragraphs 5.6.2 and 5.6.3.

5.6.6 It is not improper for a member to charge a client a lower fee than has previously been charged for similar services, provided the quality of the work does not suffer.

5.6.7 The following guidance relates to the charging of contingency or percentage fees:

(i) Professional services or the nature of financial reporting should not be offered or rendered to a client under an arrangement whereby no fee will be charged unless a specified finding or result is obtained or when the fee is otherwise contingent upon the findings or results of such services;

(ii) Fees should not be regarded as being contingent if fixed by a court or other public authority;

(iii) Fees may be waived in certain circumstances, without constituting contingency fees.

5.6.8 Fees charged on a percentage or similar basis will normally be regarded as contingent fees. In some circumstances fees cannot realistically be agreed in advance. These include assignments where by custom the fee is based on a percentage of realisation or a percentage of distribution, or where to charge a fee otherwise than on a contingency basis could deprive a potential client of professional assistance since in many cases the capacity of the client to pay may be dependent upon the success or failure of the client's venture. Similarly, in the case of a debt recovery service a flexed fee, quoted in advance, could represent such a high proportion of the recoverable debt that the client would not make use of the service.

5.6.9 The foregoing paragraphs relate to fees as distinct from reimbursement of expenses. Out-of-pocket expenses, in particular travelling expenses attribute directly to the professional services performed for a particular client, would normally be charged to that client in addition to the professional fees.

5.6.10 It is in the best interest of both the client and the member that the basis on which fees are computed and any billing arrangements are clearly defined in writing within the letter of engagement to help in avoiding misunderstandings concerning fees.

5.7 Activities incompatible with the practice of public accountancy

5.7.1 Members in public practice should not concurrently engage in any business, occupation or activity which impairs or might impair their integrity, objectivity or independence, or the good reputation of the profession, and therefore would be incompatible with the rendering of public accountancy services.

5.7.2 Public accountancy services cover a wide range of activities including accounting, auditing, taxation, management consulting and financial management services. The rendering of two or more types of such services concurrently will not by itself impair integrity, objectivity or independence.

5.7.3 The simultaneous engagement in another business, occupation or activity unrelated to public accountancy services which has the effect of not allowing the member properly to conduct a professional practice in accordance with the fundamental ethical principles of the accountancy profession should be regarded as inconsistent with the practice of public accountancy.

5.8 Clients' monies

5.8.1 In most countries there are legal duties imposed on those in public practice who hold clients' monies, including the Financial Services Act 1986. Members operating in the UK cannot hold investment business clients' monies as defined in the UK Financial Services Act 1986 unless they are regulated under authorisation schemes in accordance with that Act.

5.8.2 Members should not hold clients' monies if there is reason to believe that they were obtained from, or are to be used for, illegal activities. (See, in particular, the reference to money laundering in paragraph 3.5.6(ii)).

5.8.3 A member in public practice entrusted with monies belonging to others should:

(i)   keep such monies separately from personal monies or monies belonging to the practice;

(ii) use such monies only for the purpose for which they are intended; and

(iii) at all times be ready to account for those monies to any persons entitled to such accounting.

5.8.4 The member should maintain one or more bank accounts for clients' monies. Such bank accounts may include a general client account into which the monies of a number of clients may be paid.

5.8.5 When a member opens a bank account for clients' monies, whether it is a general client account or a separate account in the name of a client, written notice in clear terms should be given to the bank stating the title and nature of the account and requiring the bank to acknowledge in writing that it accepts the terms of the notice. Provided this procedure is followed, no question is likely to arise, in the event of the bankruptcy of the member, of set-off by the bank against the other accounts of the member or of sequestration of the amounts held in clients' accounts by a Trustee in Bankruptcy for the benefit of the general creditors.

5.8.6 Clients' monies received by a member should be deposited without delay to the credit of a client account, or, if in the form of documents of title to money or documents of title which can be converted into money, be safeguarded against unauthorised use.

5.8.7 Monies may only be drawn from a client account on the instructions of the client or for the benefit of the client.

5.8.8 Money shall not be withdrawn from a client bank account for or towards payment of fees payable by the client to the member unless:

(i)   the precise amount thereof has been agreed by the client or has been finally determined by a court or arbitrator; or

(ii) the fees have been accurately calculated in accordance with formula agreed in writing by the client on the basis of which the amount thereof can be determined; or,

(iii) thirty days have elapsed since the date of delivery to the client of a statement showing the details of the work undertaken and the client has not questions the amount therein specified as due.

5.8.9 Payments to or on behalf of a client from the client's account shall not exceed the balance standing to the credit of the client.

5.8.10 Where it seems likely that the client's monies will remain on client account for a significant period of time (in excess of two months) and the balance is in excess of £2000 or its equivalent, the member should at the time of receipt of the funds and with the concurrence of the client, place such monies in an interest bearing account in the client's name.

5.8.11 All interest earned on an individual client's monies should be credited to the client.

5.8.12 Members should keep such books of account as will enable them at any time to establish clearly their dealings with clients' monies in general and the monies of each individual client in particular. A statement of account should be provided to clients at least once a year.

5.9   Changes in a professional appointment

5.9.1 Clients have the right to choose their professional advisers, and to change to others if they wish. Members engaging in practice have the right to choose for whom they act. Nevertheless, it is necessary in the interest of both the public, and the existing and prospective advisers, that a member who is asked to act by a prospective client in respect of a recurring reporting assignment, accounting services, or taxation compliance work, should communicate with the existing appointee. Likewise the latter must reply promptly as to any considerations which might affect the prospective adviser's decision whether or not to accept appointment. Where there is no existing adviser, the procedures apply equally to any previous adviser.

5.9.2 Members should undertake the same procedures with non-members as they would with members.

5.9.3 Members invited to undertake professional work additional and related to that being carried out by another professional adviser should consult paragraph 5.11.1 (below).

5.9.4 Communication is meant to ensure that all relevant facts are known to the member considering accepting appointment, who, having considered them, is able to reach a responsible decision whether or not to accept the appointment.

5.9.5 It should be emphasised that the decision whether or not an appointment can be accepted is that of the prospective appointee. There is no procedure of "professional clearance" whereby the existing adviser can decide to give or withhold any permission to act. It is open to the existing adviser to complain to the AAT if he or she believes that a successor has accepted appointment without giving due weight to the existing adviser's reply.

5.9.6 Communication of the facts to a prospective adviser does not relieve the existing adviser of his or her duty to continue to press on the client his or her views on any technical or ethical matters which may have led him or her into dispute with the client.

5.9.7 The appropriate procedure for any member who is invited to act in succession to another adviser/member, whether the change-over is at the instance of the client or of the existing adviser is to:

(i) explain to the prospective client that the member has a professional duty to communicate with the existing adviser;

(ii) request the client to confirm the proposed change in appointment to the existing adviser, and authorise the latter to co-operate with the member as the prospective successor;

(iii) write to the existing adviser in respect of the latter's involvement with the client, requesting disclosure of any issue or circumstance which might be relevant to the proposed successor's decision to accept or decline appointment.

5.9.8 After these procedural steps have been taken, the proposed successor should consider, in the light of the information received from the existing adviser or from any other source, including any conclusions reached following discussion with the client, whether :-

(i) to accept the appointment;

(ii) accept it only having addressed any representations made by the existing adviser; or

(iii) to decline it.

5.9.9 The fact that the existing adviser's fees have not been paid is not of itself a reason for a prospective appointee to refuse to act.

5.9.10 The proposed successor should treat in confidence any information provided by the existing adviser, save to the extent that he or she needs to disclose matters necessary to carry out the assignment.

5.9.11 The appropriate procedure for any member or firm which receives a communication from a proposed successor is to:

(i) answer promptly any communications from the proposed successor about the client's affairs; and either

(ii) advise the proposed successor whether there are any issues or circumstances of which the latter ought to be aware, giving an adequate explanation of the issues or circumstances;

or

(iii) confirm to the proposed successor that there are no such issues or circumstances.

5.9.12 It is good practice for both the proposed successor and the existing adviser to record in writing any discussions which have taken place between them as to issues or circumstances.

5.9.13 If the proposed successor has received no answer to his or her enquiry as to issues or circumstances, he or she should write to the existing appointee, by Recorded Delivery service, stating his or her intention to accept the appointment unless a reply is received within a specific reasonable period. The proposed successor is entitled to assume that silence on the part of the existing appointee indicates that the latter has no adverse comment to make. A member who accepts appointment in such circumstances is not precluded from complaining to the previous appointee's professional body that the previous adviser failed to respond to his or her enquiry letter.

5.9.14 Defamation

Counsel has advised that under UK law (and that of certain other common-law based legal systems), an existing adviser who communicates to a potential successor matters damaging to the client or to any individuals concerned with the client's business will have a strong measure of protection were any action for defamation to be brought against him or her, in that the communication is likely to be protected by what is called "qualified privilege". This means that the existing appointee should not be liable to pay damages for defamatory statements even if they should turn out to be untrue, provided that they are made without what the law regards as "malice". There is little likelihood of an adviser being held to have acted "maliciously" provided that:

(i)   he or she states only what he or she sincerely believes to be true; and

(ii) he or she avoids making reckless allegations against a client or connected individuals which he or she could have no reason for believing to be true.

5.9.15 Succession Following Vacancy due to Death etc.

A member who is invited to accept appointment on the death of a sole practitioner should endeavour to obtain such information as may be needed from the deceased's alternate (where appointed), the administrators of the deceased's estate, or other available sources.

5.10   Co-operation with a successor

5.10.1 An existing adviser should deal promptly with any reasonable request for the transfer or books and papers, but as to the exercise or a lien over books and papers where fees are outstanding see paragraph 6.2.1. Members should be aware that the courts have held that no lien can exist over books or documents of a registered company which, either by statute or by articles of association of the company, have to be available for public inspection. In case of doubt, members should consult a solicitor prior to exercising a lien.

5.10.2 The incoming adviser often needs to ask his or her predecessor for information as to the client's affairs, lack of which might prejudice the client's interests. Such information should be promptly given, and unless there is a good reason to the contrary such as a significant amount of work involved, no charge should be made.

5.11   Additional related work

A member invited to undertake recurring or non-recurring work which is additional and related to continuing work carried out by an existing professional adviser, should notify the latter of the work that the member has been asked to undertake, unless the client provides acceptable reasons why the other adviser should not be informed. The member should be aware of the risks involved in undertaking work without the advantage of having communicated with other advisers.

5.12   Obtaining professional work

5.12.1 Subject to the guidance which follows, a member may seek publicity for his or her services, achievements and products and may advertise those services, achievements and products in any way or by any means consistent with the dignity of the profession, in that he or she should not project an image inconsistent with that of a professional person committed to high ethical and technical standards. A practice and its principals are responsible for any promotional activities carried out by its principals or employees on the firm's behalf.

5.12.2 Advertising

(i) Advertisements must comply with the local law and in the UK should conform as appropriate with the requirements of the British code of Advertising Practice, and the ITC and Radio Authority Code of Advertising Standards and Practice, in particular as to legality, decency, clarity, honesty and truthfulness;

(ii) The considerations set out above are of equal application to other promotional material, and to letterheads, invoices and similar practice documents;

(iii) If reference is made in promotional material to fees or the basis on which fees are calculated, the greatest care should be taken to ensure that such reference does not mislead as to:

■ the precise services to be covered; and

■ the basis of current and future fees.

(iv) Where members seek to make comparisons in their promotional material between their practices or services (including fees) and those of others, great care will be required. In particular, members should ensure that such comparisons;

■ are objective and not misleading

■ relate to the same services

■ are factual and verifiable, and

■ do not discredit or denigrate the practice or services of others.

(v) Particular care is needed in relation to claims of size or quality. For example, it is impossible to know whether a claim to be "the largest firm" in an area is a reference to the number of partners or staff, the number of offices or the amount of fee income. A claim to be "the best firm" is subjective and incapable of substantiation, and should be avoided;

(vi) A member may offer a free consultation at which levels of fees are discussed.

5.12.3 Disparaging statements

Promotional material may contain any factual statement, the truth of which a member is able to justify, but should not make disparaging references to, or disparaging comparisons with, the services of others.

5.12.4 Harassment

A member should never promote or seek to promote services in such a way, or to such an extent, as to amount to harassment of a potential client. This is likely to deter the potential client, rather than otherwise. In the event of a complaint or harassment the burden of demonstrating that approaches of a repetitive and direct nature did not amount to harassment is likely to rest with the member.

5.12.5 Introductions and commissions

A member should not give, share or offer any commission, fee or reward to a third party (other than an employee) in return for the introduction of a client unless the client is aware of the arrangements with that third party and, in particular, with regard to payment for introductions, and

(i)   either the third party is a member of a body which is governed by ethical standards comparable to these Guidelines, or

(ii) the third party complies with ethical standards comparable to those set out in these Guidelines and the member accepts responsibility for ensuring that that introduction is carried out in accordance with such standards.

5.12.6 Clients of a former employer

A member should have regard to the bad will which is likely to result from soliciting the client of an employer whose service they have recently left. A member should act professionally and with integrity in this respect.

5.12.7 Although advertising in accordance with this section is permitted by the AAT, Affiliates and students must not make any reference to the AAT when advertising their services.

5.13   Names and letterheads of practices

For the purpose of this section the term 'letterhead' means any part of the practice's notepaper and documents used by the practice for communicating with clients and other parties and includes advertisements and facsimile material.

5.13.1 A practice name should be consistent with the dignity of the profession in the sense that it should not project an image inconsistent with that of a professional practice bound to high ethical and technical standards.

5.13.2 A practice name must comply with partnership and company law as appropriate, and, in the UK, with the Business Names Act 1985.

5.13.3 A practice name should not be misleading, eg:

(i)   A practice with a limited number of offices should not describe itself on international merely on the grounds that one of them is overseas;

(ii) It would be misleading if there was a real risk that the practice name could be confused with the name of another practice, even if the member(s) of the practice could lay justifiable claim to the name;

(iii) It has been the custom of the profession for members to practice under a name based on the names of past or present members of the practice itself or of a practice with which it has merged or amalgamated. A practice name so derived will usually by in conformity with this guidance.

5.13.4 Letterheads, documents and other stationery, including, so far as applicable, nameplates, used by the practice should meet the following criteria:

(i)   They should be of an acceptable professional standard;

(ii) They must comply with legal requirements as to names of partners, principals and other participants, and with Article 20(B) of the Association's Memorandum and Articles which prohibits the use of a member's designatory letters in the name of the practice;

(iii) They should not identify any service provided by the practice as being of a specialised nature, unless a member can clearly demonstrate expertise in that particular area.

6.   Legal Considerations

6.1   Ownership of books and records

6.1.1   The rules concerning the ownership of books and records as between a client and a professional person engaged by the client to perform agreed services derive, in the UK, mainly from a combination of statute law and case law. The following paragraphs summarise the principal points on which members may require guidance. It is however stressed that before entering into contracts with clients, all members should inform themselves of the local legal position and take steps to ensure that the engagement letter covers, as far as reasonably possible, the respective rights and responsibilities.

6.1.2   Where particular documents and records are not owned by the member they generally belong to the client. In determining whether documents and records belong to the member the following considerations apply:

(i)   the nature of the contract between the member and the client usually as evidenced in an engagement letter;

(ii) the capacity in which the member acts in relation to the client;

(iii) the purpose for which the documents and records exist or are brought into being;

(iv) local law.

6.1.3   As a general rule, under UK and other common-law based systems, where the member is acting as a principal (and not as an agent) in relation to the client, only documents brought into being by the member on the specific instructions of the client belong to the client. Documents prepared, acquired or brought into being by the member, solely for the member's own purpose as a principal, belong to the member. At times however the member may be acting as an agent for a client in which case any documents will generally be the property of the client.

6.1.4   In audit assignments, for example all documents prepared by the auditor solely for the purpose of carrying out the audit belong under UK law to the auditor. Whilst AAT members may be involved in audit work, they are reminded that they are not permitted to act as auditors for limited companies or charities unless appropriately registered to do so, in the case of the UK, with the appropriate Recognised Professional Body.

6.1.5   In accountancy work the question of ownership will depend on the nature of the work. Accounting records and financial statements prepared for a client belong, under UK law to the client. A member's working papers belong to the member.

6.1.6   In taxation work, the documents will normally belong to the client.

6.1.7   Where tax, investment or other advice is given to a client, the written advice, including supporting papers belongs, under UK law, to the client but a member's working papers belong to the member.

6.1.8   Letters received by the member from the client, copies of letters from the member to the client and notes made by the member of discussions with the client belong, under UK law, to the member.

6.1.9   Ownership of copies of communications between the member and third parties depends on the relationship with the client. The guidance in paragraph 6.1.5 above will generally apply to such communications. If the member is acting as agent for the client (eg. in tax correspondence) letters to the member and copies of the member's letters to the third part belong, under UK law to the client. However, where the member acts as principal the communications will belong to the member.

6.2   Lien

6.2.1   When a member has, in the UK, carried out work on the documents of a client and the bill the member has rendered has not been paid, the member will have, under UK law, what is called a "particular lien" over those documents. This means that the member will be able to retain possession of the documents until his or her fees have been paid.

6.2.2   The member will have a right of lien where all three of the following conditions exist:

(i)   the documents retained are the property of the client and not of a third party;

(ii)   the documents have come into the member's possession by proper means; and

(iii)   work has been done by the member on the documents, and the member has rendered an adequately detailed fee note, and the fees are outstanding in respect of that work. For example, a member is not able to exercise a lien in respect of documents of the same client on which past, remunerated work was carried out, or where fees are outstanding on the part of a company, but the work was carried out on documents which are the personal property of a director. Further, special rules apply in relation to the statutory books and accounting records of companies, and where documents are claimed by an Administrator or Liquidator of a company, or the Official Receiver or a Trustee in Bankruptcy. Further guidance can be obtained from the AAT or from a solicitor.

6.3   Retention of books, working papers and other documents

6.3.1   The following paragraphs summarise the general position in the UK regarding the retention of books, working papers and similar documents.

6.3.2   There is a general principle that after the passage of a given period of time an action may not be brought before the courts. The law requires that persons with a legitimate cause should make their claim within a reasonable time.

6.3.3   A number of statutes lay down specific periods of time within which actions must be commenced. However, where statutes do not specify time limits the Limitation Act of 1980 sets out the general position on time limits, ie:

(i) twelve years for actions upon a speciality (a contract under seal or an obligation under seal securing a debt) or a judgement given by the courts;

(ii) six years for actions based upon a simple contract or tort, or three years from the earliest date on which the plaintiff or any person in whom the cause of action was vested before that person first had both the knowledge required for bringing an action for damages in respect of the relevant damage and a right to bring such action subject to a maximum period of fifteen years.

The result of this is that members should retain books, working papers and other documents for the period of limitation, ie. no less than six years. Since a disaffected client or other person could issue a writ against the firm before the end of the expiry of the six year period, and delay serving it for up to a year, seven years might, in fact, be the most prudent retention period.

6.3.4 Taxation records should be retained for 8 years.

6.3.5 Members should note that there may be significant differences between UK law and the law of other countries where the time limits quoted above will not necessarily apply.

6.3.6 Members who are in doubt about the time limits applicable to the retention of books, working papers or other documents should consult their legal advisers.

6.4 Professional liability of members

6.4.1 The following guidance is concerned only with the liability for professional negligence which a member may incur because of an act or default by the member or an employee or associate of the member which results in financial loss to a person to whom a duty of care is owed. It does not deal with liability arising from other causes (for example criminal acts, breaches of trust or breaches of contract, other than the negligent performance of its terms, and certain heads of liability arising by statute independently of contract). Because of the need to keep the ethical guidelines to reasonable proportions the guidance is published in summary form. Members should however be aware of the number of cases in recent years where substantial sums have been claimed from accountants in damages for negligence. When entering into contracts with clients therefore, where there appears to be any doubt about the extent of the member's liability, the member is recommended to seek legal advice. Although the guidance which follows is framed in terms of UK law, similar considerations will apply in most legal regimes.

6.4.2 Before carrying out any work for a client a member should ensure that the exact duties to be performed and in particular any significant matters to be excluded have been agreed with the client in writing by a letter of engagement or otherwise. If the member is asked to perform any additional duties at a later date these should also be defined in writing.

6.4.3 In giving informal advice at the request of a client, or advice which must necessarily be based on incomplete information, a member should make it clear that such advice is subject to limitations and that consideration in depth may lead to a revision of the advice given.

6.4.4 When publishing documents generally a member may find it advantageous to include in the document a clause disclaiming liability. Such a clause cannot however be relied on in all circumstances. For example, a court might hold that such a disclaimer represented an unreasonable exclusion of liability.

6.4.5   When submitting unaudited accounts or financial statements to the client a member should ensure that any special purpose for which the documents have been prepared is recorded on their face, and in appropriate cases should introduce a clause recording that the document is confidential and has been prepared solely for the private use of the client.

6.4.6   When giving a reference to a third party with regard to future transactions (eg. payment of rent) a member should state that it is given without financial responsibility on the part of the member.

6.4.7   Where the circumstances appear to warrant it because of the complexity of an assignment or otherwise a member should either seek specialist advice or suggest that the client should do so.

6.4.8   The attention of all members in practice is drawn to the need to maintain an adequate level of Professional Indemnity Insurance cover in accordance with the scheme for members in practice. Professional Indemnity Insurance is strongly recommended for student members who undertake self-employed work.

Appendix 2

Sample Letter of Engagement

This is an example of a letter of engagement that an accountant would send out to a client before commencing an assignment. In this case the assignment is for the preparation of the year-end accounts for AKL Home Improvements.

The content of a letter of engagement can vary widely depending on the nature of the assignment. For example, the letter of engagement for a tax client would refer to the fact that the accountant was acting as an agent for the client.

It is also worth noting that different accounting practices will vary the wording of the letter of engagement that they send to the client, depending on their preferred style, but the sections covered should be broadly the same.

LETTER OF ENGAGEMENT

Dear Client,

The purpose of this letter is to set out the basis on which **Jacques and Khan Accountants** are engaged as your accountants and the respective responsibilities of yourselves and us.

Nature of the assignment

You have instructed us to prepare your financial statements for the year(s) ended 30th September, 2007, and subsequent years. The next section covers the detailed responsibilities that we undertake.

Responsibilities of the accountants

1.1 We shall compile the annual accounts based on the accounting records maintained by you and the information and explanations given to us by you. We shall compile draft annual accounts for your approval. We shall plan our work on the basis that no report is required by statute or regulation for the year, unless you inform us in writing to the contrary.

1.2 Our work as the compilers of the annual accounts will not be an audit of the accounts in accordance with Auditing Standards. Consequently our work will not provide any assurance that the accounting records or the accounts are free from material misstatement, whether caused by fraud, other irregularities or error.

1.3 We shall report, with any variations that we consider may be necessary, that in accordance with your instructions, we have compiled without carrying out an audit, the accounts from the accounting records of the business and from the information and explanations supplied to us.

1.4 We have a professional duty to compile accounts which conform to generally accepted accounting principles. Where we identify that the accounts do not conform to accepted accounting principles, or if the accounting policies adopted are not immediately apparent, this will be made clear in our report, if it is not clear in the accounts.

1.5 As part of our normal procedures we may request you to provide written confirmation of any information or explanations given to us orally during the course of our work.

Your responsibility

2.1   You have undertaken to make available to us, as and when required, all the accounting records and related financial information necessary for the compilation of the accounts. You will make full disclosure to us of all relevant information. The accounts need to be approved by you before we are able to issue our report.

2.2   You are responsible for ensuring that, to the best of your knowledge and belief, financial information, whether used by the business or for the accounts, is reliable. You are also responsible for ensuring that the activities of the business are conducted honestly and that its assets are safeguarded, and for establishing arrangements designed to deter fraudulent or other dishonest conduct and to detect any that occurs.

2.3   You are responsible for ensuring that the business complies with the laws and regulations applicable to its activities, and for establishing arrangements designed to prevent any non-compliance with laws and regulations and to detect any that occur.

Timetable

A private company is required to file its accounts at Companies House within 10 months of the year end. The company will be liable to a fine if it fails to do so. In order to avoid this we will produce statutory accounts suitable for filing, within the required period, provided all your records are complete and presented to us within six months of the year end, and all subsequent queries are promptly and satisfactorily answered.

Fees

Our fees are computed on the basis of time spent on your affairs and the responsibility and skill involved by the partners and staff of this firm. Unless otherwise agreed, our fees will be billed at appropriate intervals during the course of the year. Unless specifically agreed, payment of our invoices is due within 7 days from the date of the invoice.

Interest will be charged on all overdue debts at the rate stated on the invoice, which is currently ....% (APR...........%) [or, at the rate for the time being applicable under the Late Payment of Commercial Debts (Interest) Act 1998, whichever is the higher].

Ownership of records

In the event of non-payment of our fees for services rendered, we may exercise a particular right of lien over the books and records in our possession and withhold the documents until such time as payment of our invoice is received in full.

Commissions or other benefits

In some circumstances, commissions or other benefits may become payable to us in respect of introductions to other professionals or transactions we arrange for you, in which case you will be notified in writing of the amount, the terms of payment and receipt of any such commissions or benefits.

Any commission received will be paid to you.

File destruction

Whilst certain documents may legally belong to you, unless you tell us not to, we intend to destroy correspondence and other papers that we store which are more than seven years old, other than documents which we think may be of continuing significance. If you require the retention of any document, you must notify us of that fact in writing.

Ethical guidelines

We are bound by the ethical guidelines of the Association of Accounting Technicians and accept instructions to act for you on the basis that we will act in accordance with those ethical guidelines.

Clients' monies

We may, from time to time, hold money on your behalf. Such money will be held in trust in a client bank account, which is segregated from the firm's funds.

If the total sum of money held on your behalf exceeds £2,000 for a period of more than 2 months, or such sum is likely to be held for more than 2 months, then the money will be placed in an interest-bearing client bank account. All interest earned on such money will be paid to you. Subject to any tax legislation, interest will be paid gross.

If there are grounds to suspect (even if we do not actually suspect) that any monies held in a client account is derived directly or indirectly from any criminal activity whatsoever, we may not release such monies until we receive permission to do so from NCIS.

Third Parties

All accounts, statements and reports prepared by us are for your exclusive use within your business or to meet specific statutory responsibilities. They should not be shown to any other party without our prior consent.

No third party shall acquire any rights pursuant to our agreement to provide professional services. .

Applicable Law

This engagement letter shall be governed by, and construed in accordance with, English law. The Courts of England shall have exclusive jurisdiction in relation to any claim, dispute or difference concerning the engagement letter and any matter arising from it. Each party irrevocably waives any right it may have to object to an action being brought in those Courts, to claim that the action has been brought in an inconvenient forum, or to claim that those Courts do not have jurisdiction.

Disclaimer

We will not be liable for any loss suffered by you or any third party as a result of our compliance with the Anti Money Laundering Legislation or any UK law or at all.

Agreement of terms

Once it has been agreed, this letter will remain effective, from one appointment to another, until it is replaced. We shall be grateful if you could confirm in writing your agreement to these terms by signing and returning the enclosed copy of this letter, or let us know if they are not in accordance with your understanding of our terms of engagement.

Yours sincerely

P Jacques   I Khan

For Jacques and Khan Accountants

I/We agree to the terms of this letter

A K Liennt

Signed for:

AKL Home Improvements

Date: 1 April 2007

Index